WebPlus Essentials
User Guide

How to Contact Us

Our main office
(UK, Europe):

The Software Centre
PO Box 2000, Nottingham,
NG11 7GW, UK

Main:

(0115) 914 2000

Registration (UK only):

(0800) 376 1989

Sales (UK only):

(0800) 376 7070

Customer Service/
Technical Support:

www.serif.com/support

General Fax:

(0115) 914 2020

North American office
(USA, Canada):

The Software Center
13 Columbia Drive, Suite 5,
Amherst NH 03031, USA

Main:

(603) 889-8650

Registration:

(800) 794-6876

Sales:

(800) 55-SERIF or 557-3743

Customer Service/
Technical Support:

www.serif.com/support

General Fax:

(603) 889-1127

Online

Visit us on the web at:

www.serif.com/

International

Please contact your local distributor/dealer. For further details please contact us
at one of our phone numbers above.

Contents

1 Welcome

Welcome!

Welcome to WebPlus Essentials from **Serif**—the easy way to get your family, club, organization, or small business on the web!

To make life so much easier, WebPlus comes with an impressive selection of **design templates**, page **navigation bars**, creative **gallery** content, and **styles** for you to use. As a result, publishing to the web to a professional standard is easily achievable for experienced and inexperienced users alike!

To make the most of pictures in your site, you can use **Image Cutout Studio** for cutting pictures out and **PhotoLab** for powerful image adjustment and effect combinations. When you're ready, share via online **photo galleries**. You simply cannot afford to miss these features!

WebPlus Essentials doesn't just stop at "static" web publishing. The real power comes when adding and managing dynamic content, such as **blogs**, **forums**, **counters**, and more. You can even make use of **E-commerce tools** for money-making shopping cart functionality.

Once you're happy with your WebPlus site, simply upload to your Serif webspace (or equivalent ISP) to share with business colleagues, customers, friends and family alike.

For a more detailed summary of what WebPlus can offer, see **Key features** (p. 4).

Registration

Don't forget to register your new copy, using the **Registration Wizard**, on the **Help** menu. That way, we can keep you informed of new developments and future upgrades!

Key features

Before you get started with WebPlus, we recommend you take the opportunity
to familiarize yourself with WebPlus key features and capabilities.

Layout

- **Multipage Design Templates**
  Make "tailored" websites based on a chosen look and color scheme in
  an instant—choose design templates from Interest, Personal,
  Community & Education, and Home Business categories, all packed
  with royalty free images for you to use. Alternatively, choose a **theme
  layout** such as Arctic or Natural on which to base your site—pick
  multiple layouts as your new pages, then simply fill picture
  placeholders with your own pictures.

- **Professional layout tools**
  Movable **rulers**, **guide lines** and a **dot grid**, as layout aids, help you
  position objects precisely; snapping jumps an object to guide or grid.
  Use **Sticky guides**, a great way of moving (in bulk) all objects
  snapped to your guide lines—move the guide and objects will follow!

- **Page control**
  Add and **remove pages** in just a few clicks of your mouse in the **Site
  tab**. Drag and drop pages within the tab to reorder sequence. Assign
  master pages to several site pages at once for time saving and greater
  design consistency.

- **Use multiple master pages!**
  For more varied page design, apply multiple master pages to a specific
  web page.

Website Essentials

- **Easy site structure**
  The hierarchical **Site tab** makes it easy to see the overall layout of
  your site.

- **Exciting Navigation Bars**
  Use **navigation bars** for site-wide page navigation. Flexible and user configurable, with a host of different design styles to choose from—share styles for a common look between navigation bars. You can also include forum and blog articles in dynamically changing navigation bar submenus. Navigation Manager controls all navigation bars from one point. Add separators between submenu items.

- **Search Engine Optimization**
  Control how search engines index your website! Include or exclude pages from indexing by using search engine sitemap or robot files—protect confidentiality while offering potential web visitors accurate search results from your site.

- **Smart Objects**
  Serif Web Resources, Serif's Smart object hosting service, offers a series of interactive site features:

  - **Forum**—Stimulates lively thread-based discussions in a full-sized window. Create multiple forums and manage independently (moderate discussions and set up user login access).

  - **User List**—offers page or site access control by management of "zonal" **user groups** (e.g., Personnel). Web visitors can self-register via a site's user login (with optional email activation).

  - **News**—For simple news announcements such as website updates or next club meeting dates.

  - **Blogs**—now add personal **profiles**, **social bookmarking links** and use **trackbacks** for inter-blog cross-referencing. Change blog appearance with different pre-defined **Visual Styles** (or use your own!). Use **Editor groups** for multi-author article publishing.

- **E-Commerce—Sell, Sell, Sell!**
  WebPlus makes the process of placing items for sale on your website quick and easy with its built-in support for E-Commerce shopping cart providers (e.g., PayPal)! Simply adding E-Commerce Forms, E-Commerce Buttons, or even a hyperlink from any WebPlus object (text, pictures or shapes) will access your chosen shopping cart. Buy Now, Add to Shopping Cart, Donation, and Subscription forms will get money moving with buying options and form validation thrown in! Sign up to shopping carts directly or adopt existing accounts.

- **RSS—News and Information Feeds on your page**
  Keep your web visitors up to date with the latest news from your
  favorite websites (BBC News, Reuters, FTSE, NASDAQ) with the
  RSS Reader Tool. Alternatively, be a news anchor yourself by
  creating your own RSS feed directly on your page—the **RSS Feed
  Tool** sets up feeds, headlines, summaries and URL links.

- **Web-ready Forms for gathering content**
  Apply forms to your web pages—use a WebForm Wizard to adopt
  ready-to-go standard forms for contact details, user
  feedback/comments, canvassing opinions, or uploading documents
  (e.g., CVs) or pictures. Use **Standard Form Objects** as building
  blocks to slash form design time! Submit form data via Web
  Resources, Serif's free form-to-email transit gateway (data goes
  straight to your email on submission) or subject data to local/remote
  scripting. Control tab order for improved form navigation.

- **No more lost customers with Google Maps!**
  Embed a Google Map directly into your "Directions" web page. Add
  your own **multiple markers** to pinpoint locations such as offices,
  depots, places of interest, and events.

- **Site Management Tools**
  Manage all your **Page/Master Page Properties**, **resources**, **fonts**,
  text, **hyperlinks**, and **anchors**—all from within WebPlus's **Site
  Manager**. Powerfully manage web pages individually, by selection, or
  apply to all pages. Site Checker detects Site Navigation, Text
  Formatting, and Form/E-commerce problems and carries out
  automatic fixes where possible.

Ease of Use

- **QuickBuilder Bar**
  The simple way to get started with WebPlus—drag pages, navigation
  bars, text frames, images, Flash content, photo galleries, or Smart
  objects directly onto the page for quick results with no prior
  knowledge of the user interface.

- **Learn WebPlus**
  The Startup Wizard's new **Learning Zone** helps you get the very best
  out of WebPlus. Tutorials, both PDF and video, are published along
  with a host of other resources and product support details.

- **Quick Publish**
  Upload and view a currently displayed page—great for live verification of individual pages as you build your website.

- **Dynamic guides**
  Align and resize objects with each other using **dynamic guide snapping**, without the need for ruler guides or precise object transforms.

Pictures

- **Import Pictures**
  Import commonly-used standard file formats, including all the latest RAW digital camera formats, Photoshop files, Microsoft HD Photo, and Serif SMF files. Import multiple images and paste one by one!

- **More picture power with Media Bar**
  No more repetitive photo importing! Keep photo content to hand in the new **Media Bar**—drag and drop from the Media Bar onto pictures to replace! Search for pictures by their metadata. Control picture sizing and alignment within its frame.

- **Stunning online Photo Galleries!**
  Wow your friends, family and colleagues with stunning Flash and JavaScript photo galleries. Various **gallery styles** offer photo navigation by selection from thumbnails, thumbnail rollovers, photo grid or photo stack. Use the Autoplay feature for looping photo slideshows. Finally, take advantage of caption support (using EXIF data)!

- **Quick Image Adjustments**
  From the Picture context toolbar, apply **adjustments** (Brightness, Contrast, fix red eye, and more) quickly or use **Edit in PhotoPlus**, which accesses Serif's award-winning photo-editing package (if installed).

- **PhotoLab for non-destructive adjustment and effect filters**
  The powerful **PhotoLab** packs a punch with an impressive selection of editable adjustments, creative, and artistic effects (pencil, water color, oil, and more). Use integrated **Straighten**, **Crop**, **Red-eye**, and **Spot-repair** tools for easy **retouching**. Apply filters to selected areas of your photo by using **brush-based masking**. **Save** adjustment/effect combinations as favorites for future use.

- **Quick-and-easy Image Cutouts**
  Image Cutout Studio makes light work of cutting out your placed pictures, directly in WebPlus. Use brushes to discard uniform backgrounds (sky, walls, etc.) or keep subjects of interest (people, objects, etc.).

- **A versatile Metafile Format**
  Import and Export Serif Metafiles (.smf), a proprietary image format with improvements to the Windows Metafile format (WMF). Better line, fill, and text definitions make them ideal for sharing graphics between Serif applications.

- **Popup Rollovers**
  Create your own simple photo gallery—show a larger version of a picture on thumbnail hover over.

Media

- **YouTube® Videos**
  Pick your favorite YouTube® videos and include them on your web page!

- **Podcasts**
  Create your own **podcast** feeds and broadcast your own audio and video episodes frequently and easily. Web visitors can subscribe with all the most popular web browsers and via on-click subscription to Google Reader®, My Yahoo!®, and Apple iTunes®.

Creativity

- **Drawing Tools**
  Design stunning vector graphics with Pencil, Pen and Straight **Line tools**, and add line endings like arrowheads, diamonds, and quills. Alternatively, the array of fully-customizable **QuickShapes** let you quickly create outlines for your designs, while **Convert to Curves**, **Crop to Shape**, and curve drawing offer complete flexibility for creating any shape imaginable! **Mesh warp envelopes** add perspective, slant, and bulge to any object. Use stroke alignment for precise positioning, align a shape or Creative text's **stroke** to the inside, outside, or center of its **path**.

- **Ready-to-use Styles**
  Choose various filter effects, glows, shadows, textures, and materials from the Styles tab. Customize the preset styles or store your own!

- **Photo-based borders**
  Exciting new ready-to-go borders can be applied around text frames, tables and pictures alike. Create and save custom borders from your own electronic border designs or scanned picture frames! The Gallery tab's **Picture frames** have the same borders already applied.

- **Joining object outlines**
  Combine QuickShapes, drawn shapes and artistic text together to create more complex outlined objects, which can still be edited further. Use **Add**, **Subtract**, **Intersect**, and **Exclude** to produce different and exciting results.

- **Transparency**
  Add transparency to your backgrounds, text frames, tables, shapes and text to achieve a truly professional look. As with color fills, you can apply **solid**, **gradient**, and **bitmap** transparencies—even create bitmap transparencies from your own image collection.

- **Intelligent Color Schemes**
  Choose from dozens of preset color schemes to change the overall appearance of your site with a single click. Use Color Scheme Designer to design your very own **custom color schemes** using spreads based on accepted color theory (**Monochromatic**, **Complementary**, **Triadic**, and more). Pick a starting base color and choose from a range of suggested and related colors—select individually or populate colors automatically for a new scheme.

- **New 2D/3D Filter Effects**
  Add stunning **reflections** of an object—great for web page titles and pictures! **Blur** any object or stroke a colored solid or gradient border around object edges (stroke with a new **Contour** fill which applies gradient fill from the inner to outer outline width). 3D effects are boosted with realistic glass-like **Transparency** control of non-reflective/reflective surfaces and multiple separately colored lights for dramatic lighting effects. All filter effects can be applied in preview mode or to the object on the page. Use the new **Shadow Tool** for on-the-page shadow control.

- **Instant 3D with On-screen Transforms**
  Transform 3D objects **in-situ** with 3D editing from a context toolbar.
  Apply multi-colored **lighting effects** (with directional control), along
  with custom **bevel** and **lathe** effect profiles to create your very own
  unique contours. **Hardware-accelerated rendering** boosts redraw
  performance (hardware dependent).

Text

- **Import Word 2007 and Open Office text documents**
  Add word processing content to any text frame without fuss! Import
  doesn't need the application to be installed locally! Use a choice of
  import converters to optimize text import.

- **Artistic and frame text**
  Have complete control over your text with WebPlus's DTP-style text
  control. Artistic text can be used to give your websites high impact—
  especially good for titling or adding to a drawn path. HTML text
  frames allow you to remain HTML compliant whereas successive
  Creative text frames can be filled automatically with text by
  AutoFlow or manual text fitting. All text has editing capabilities
  compatible with top of the range word processors!

- **Text Frames**
  Compose story text in HTML or Creative **text frames** then easily
  position or size the frame to suit; connected Creative text frames host
  the same story text and can be filled automatically by **AutoFlow** or
  manual text fitting. Separate crop and wrap outlines mean you have
  greater control over where text flows and how it appears. Import,
  paste, export text in **Unicode** format... design with a foreign-language
  or special fonts and characters. Text paths also benefit from intelligent
  text fitting.

- **Fonts**
  Substitute missing fonts when opening third-party projects. View
  your currently installed font set in the Fonts tab, including those most
  recently assigned to text, favorite fonts, and those considered
  Websafe. Hover over a listed font for an "in-situ" **font preview** of
  your selected text—simply click to apply the new font if you like it!
  Easily **swap** all selected instances of a common font for another font
  in one fell swoop!

- **Tables and Calendars**
  Choose from a range of preset formats or design your own table. Use the convenient Table context toolbar to sort data, format cells, and choose from a wide range of functions for **spreadsheet calculations** (use absolute cell references). **Calendars** are table-based for enhanced functionality, and support Year update, inline personal events, and public holidays!

- **Find & Replace**
  Search through story text for words and phrases but also text attributes, particular fonts, colors, special characters (Unicode), regular expressions, and words at specific positions in sentences.

Web Publishing

- **Previewing your work**
  Test drive your new web page or your entire site in a choice of different installed web browsers.

- **Publish your site**
  Publish to a local folder or upload directly to your ISP via FTP; upload any new or edited pages incrementally.

- **Website hosting with Serif**
  Publish your site with **Serif**! Combine simple sign-up, different levels of service, and no-fuss publishing for the ideal hosting solution. Set up via your Serif Web Resources account while managing access control, forums, blogs, and other Smart objects at the same time.

Installation

System Requirements

Minimum:

- Pentium PC with DVD/CD drive and mouse

- Microsoft Windows® XP (32 bit), Windows® Vista, or Windows® 7 operating system

- 512MB RAM

- 510MB free hard disk space

- 1024 x 600 monitor resolution

- Internet Explorer 5.5 (6.0 or above for Smart object use)

Additional disk resources and memory are required when editing large and/or complex images.

Optional:

- Windows-compatible printer

- TWAIN-compatible scanner and/or digital camera

- 3D Accelerated graphics card with DirectX 9 (or above) or OpenGL support

- .NET 2.0 for text import filters (Word 2007 + OpenOffice) (installed by default)

- Internet account and connection required for web publishing and accessing online resources

- Adobe® Flash® Player 9.0 or above to view Learning Zone resources

First-time install

To install WebPlus, simply insert the Program CD into your DVD/CD drive. The AutoRun feature automatically starts the Setup process. Just answer the on-screen questions to install the program.

Re-install

To re-install the software or to change the installation at a later date, select **Settings/Control Panel** from the Windows Start menu and then click on the **Add/Remove Programs** icon. Make sure the WebPlus Essentials Program CD is inserted into your CD/DVD drive, click the **Install...** button and then simply follow the on-screen instructions.

2 Getting Started

Startup Wizard

Once WebPlus has been installed, you'll be ready to start. Setup adds a Serif **WebPlus Essentials** item to the **(All) Programs** submenu of the Windows **Start** menu.

- Use the Windows **Start** button to pop up the Start Menu, click on **All Programs** and then click the WebPlus item.

The Startup Wizard presents several choices:

The options are self explanatory, where site creation can be made from scratch or from a pre-supplied design template. Previously saved sites can be opened or non-WebPlus web pages can be imported into your site from file or URL.

- **Start New Site**, to create your own site from scratch.

- **Use Design Template**, to create an instant site from a pre-designed template.

- **Open Saved Site**, to open a previously saved WebPlus site.

- **WebPlus hosting**, to host your published WebPlus site with Serif.

- **Learning Zone**, to access videos, tutorials, support information, and more.

Use the **Choose Workspace** drop-down menu to choose your workspace appearance (i.e., Studio tab positions, tab sizes, and show/hide tab status). You can adopt the default workspace profile <**Default Profile**>, the last used profile <**Current Profile**>, a range of profile presets, or a workspace profile you have previously saved.

> As you click on different profiles from the menu, your workspace will preview each tab layout in turn.

The Startup Wizard is displayed by default when you launch WebPlus. You can switch it off via the **Don't show this wizard again** check box on the Startup Wizard screen, or on again via the **Use Startup Wizard** check box in **Tools>Options...** (use Options>General menu option).

Creating a site using a design template

WebPlus comes complete with a whole range of categorized design templates which will speed you through the creation of all kinds of websites.

Each template offers:

- **Complementary design**—Professionally designed layout with high-visual impact.

- **Schemes**—choose a named color scheme to apply a specific look and feel (e.g., Atlantis).

- **Page selection**—select some or all template pages (e.g., Home, Products, About Us, etc.) to base your new site on.

Design templates come in two types—**theme layouts**, where you pick your own pictures, or **ready-to-go templates** which are already populated with pictures.

Arctic   Clean   Decor

Theme layouts
These offer a choice of themes (e.g., Arctic) on which to base your site; you'll get picture placeholders instead of actual pictures. Simply add your own pictures to placeholders and personalize placeholder text, then publish.

Cafe   Campsite   Painter & Decorator

Ready-to-go templates
These are categorized templates containing royalty-free pictures which can be adopted to fast-track you to your completed website. You just need to personalize placeholder text, then publish.

Template categories include Interest, Personal, Community & Education, and Home Business.

To create a site using a design template:

1. Launch WebPlus, or choose **Startup Wizard...** from the **File** menu, to display the Startup Wizard.

2. Select **Use Design Template**.

3.   From the dialog, select a theme or template design from the main pane.

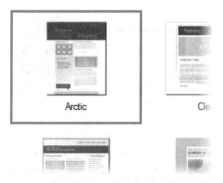

Templates are grouped into subject-based categories; use the scroll bar or collapse a category to reveal more options (click the ⊟ button next to the category name). The right-hand pane refreshes to display thumbnails of that template's available pages.

4.   From the right-hand pane, decide which pages you wish to be part of your site. Check or uncheck under each page to select, or click **Select All** to select all pages (click **Deselect All** to clear the current selection).

5.   Pick a **Color Scheme** from the drop-down list at the top of the dialog (for theme layouts, the first three schemes are designed specifically for that layout). The page thumbnails refresh to reflect the new page's appearance. For a closer look, use the Zoom In/Zoom Out buttons or Zoom slider at the bottom of the dialog.

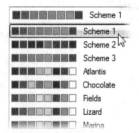

6.   Click **Open**.

The site opens to the first (Home) page, with the Studio's Site tab displayed on the right, showing the various pages that comprise the site in its Site Structure tree.

★ As each template is color schemed, you can swap the underlying scheme, and the site's appearance, for another scheme at any time!

Notes

★ Some templates contain Smart objects (see p. 267) such as newsletter sign ups and polls. As Smart objects are stored in Serif Web Resources they have to be associated with a valid Serif customer account. If you want to make use of the Smart object (if unwanted just delete them), double-click it and login to Serif Web Resources; this will associate the object to your account.

★ Once you're working in WebPlus you can easily adopt additional pages from **any** template to add style variation to your site—for instance, you could create web pages with a set look and feel, but a separate members-only area could adopt a different look entirely by adding another templates' pages. See Adding, removing, and rearranging pages on p. 34 for more details.

Starting a site from scratch

Although design templates can simplify your design choices, you can just as easily start out from scratch with a new, blank site.

To start a new site from scratch using the Startup Wizard:

- Launch WebPlus, and select **Create>Start New Site**.

The new site opens with a blank page using default page properties.

★ If you click ▦ **Cancel** (or press **Escape**) from the Startup Wizard, you'll get the same result.

To start a new site during your WebPlus session:

- Choose **New** from the **File** menu.

To help you quickly build a site from scratch, WebPlus offers the **QuickBuilder Bar**. The tab hosts commonly used objects and features which can be introduced onto your web page by drag-and-drop, avoiding the need to initially understand the range of WebPlus toolbars.

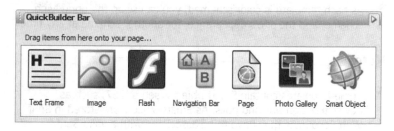

Opening an existing site

You can open an existing WebPlus site from the Startup Wizard, via the **Standard** toolbar, or via the **File** menu.

To open an existing WebPlus site (Startup Wizard):

1. Select the **Open Saved Site** option. In the Documents pane of the **Open Saved Work** dialog, you'll see either your computer's folder structure for navigation to your sites (Folders tab) or a list of most recently used sites (History tab). Preview thumbnails or site details can be shown in the adjacent pane depending on your current view.

2. Click a file name or sample, then click **Open**. The site opens to the first (Home) page.

To open an existing WebPlus site (during WebPlus session):

1. Click 📂 **Open** on the **Standard** toolbar.

2. In the Open dialog, select the folder and file name and click the **Open** button.

To revert to the saved version of an open site:

- Choose **Revert** from the **File** menu.

Font substitution

WebPlus supports automatic font substitution as you open a WebPlus site which has fonts which are not stored on your computer. The dialog that shows also lets you manually substitute a missing font if necessary. See online Help for more details.

Working with more than one site

If you have multiple websites open at the same time it's easy to jump between them using different methods.

Click on a Window tab at the top of the workspace to make it active (e.g., Design657.wpp).

Alternatively, you can select the name of a currently open site from the **Window** menu. Unsaved websites are indicated by an asterisk; the currently active site is shown with a tick. In the example above, the Design657.wpp site is active and also unsaved.

Saving your site

To save your work:

- Click  **Save** on the **Standard** toolbar.

- To save under a different name, choose **Save As...** from the **File** menu.

An unsaved site will have an asterisk after its name shown in either its Window tab or on the **Window** menu.

3 Developing Sites and Pages

Understanding site structure and navigation

Unlike a printed publication, a website doesn't depend on a linear page sequence. When designing a site, it makes more sense to think of the site in spatial terms, with a **structure** like that of a museum which people will explore. You can generally assume that your visitors will come in through the "front door" (the Home page)—but where they go after that depends on the links you've provided. These **navigation** pathways are like corridors that connect the various rooms of the museum. It's up to you as the "architect" to develop a sensible arrangement of pages and links so that visitors can find their way around easily, without getting lost.

In WebPlus, you can use the **Site Structure tree** to visually map out the structure of your site and then add navigation bars—that dynamically adapt to the structure you've defined.

Site structure

Unlike the museum in our analogy, the "structure" of a website has nothing to do with its physical layout, or where pages are stored. Rather, it's a way of logically arranging the content on the site so that visitors have an easier time navigating through it. One of the most useful organizing principles—which WebPlus strongly reinforces—is an "inverted tree" structure that starts with the Home page and then branches out to other pages. To the visitor navigating your site, this arrangement presents your content in a familiar, hierarchical way, structured into **sections** and **levels**.

- A **section** is a content category, for example "Who's Who?," "Products," or "Links." The various major sections are typically listed on the site's Home page in a navigation bar. Ideally, each page on the site belongs to a particular section. And unless there's only one page in a given section, the section will have its own main page, which usually serves as a menu for subsidiary pages.

- The **level** is the number of steps (i.e., jumps) a given page is removed from the Home page. The Home page will always reside at Level 1, normally along with main section menu pages. This allows navigation bars to work easily and automatically. Pages one step "below" the section menu pages reside at Level 2, and so on.

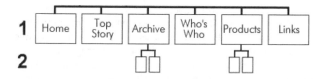

In WebPlus, the Site Structure tree (in the Site tab) provides a visual aid that lets you organize the content on your site into sections and levels—in other words as a hierarchy of parent pages branching to child pages. Here's how the same structure might appear in the WebPlus Site Structure tree:

The Site Structure tree makes it easy to visualize relationships between pages and lay out your site in a way that makes sense for the content you have to offer. Of course, a website is truly an interconnected web of pages, and the tree structure doesn't prevent you from installing links between any two pages. But it does expose the major pathways within your site—up, down, and sideways. Logical section/level design makes your site easier to navigate, and WebPlus makes it simple to create **navigation bars** that mirror your site structure and help guide your visitors along those "main roads."

Incidentally, WebPlus also supports offsite links which can be inserted into the Site Structure as for any other page. Either page entry is slightly different in design to a standard web page to indicate that it points to a location outside of the website.

As an example, compare a standard web page "Sales" with the offsite link "Member's forum."

Navigation

In WebPlus, adding navigation between your web pages is easy with navigation bars, each pre-programmed to understand your site structure, making it easy to design a site that's simple to navigate. You simply select one from the Web Objects toolbar and WebPlus does the rest!

For example, here's a navigation bar we selected for the site shown in the main tree above. The buttons provide links to the Home and section menu pages (all at Level 1) and popup menus that link to child pages (Level 2 in this case).

For more information, see Adding navigation bars on p. 41.

Understanding pages and master pages

Pages are the basic unit of web design. WebPlus lets you structure your site's content by arranging pages into a branching "tree," which in turn helps visitors navigate through the site. Looking at individual pages from a design standpoint, each WebPlus page has a "foreground" **page** and a "background" **master page**.

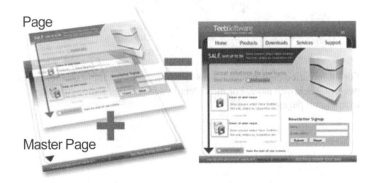

Master pages are part of the structure of your WebPlus site, and provide a flexible way to store background elements that you would like to appear on more than one page—for example a logo, background, border design, or navigation bar. The key concept here is that a particular master page is typically shared by multiple pages, as illustrated below. By placing a design element on a master page and then assigning several pages to use that master page, you ensure that all the pages incorporate that element. Of course, each individual page can have its own elements.

The Studio's **Site tab** includes an upper Master Pages section with icons for each master page, and a lower Site Structure in the Pages window that provides feedback indicating which master page is being used by each of your web pages:

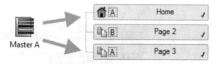

For more varied page designs across you site, you can apply multiple master pages to each web page. For more details, see Adding, removing, and rearranging pages on p. 34.

Viewing pages

The WebPlus workspace consists of a "page" area and a surrounding "pasteboard" area.

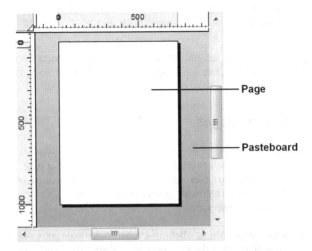

The **page** area is where you put the text, graphics, and other elements that you want to appear on your final web page. The **pasteboard** is where you generally keep elements that are being prepared or waiting to be positioned on the page area. When you publish your site from the WebPlus site, anything which overlaps the page area appears, while anything entirely on the pasteboard does not. The pasteboard is shared by all pages and master pages, and it's useful for copying or moving objects between pages.

To move or copy an object between pages via the pasteboard:

1. Drag the object from the source page onto the pasteboard (hold down the **Ctrl** key to copy).

2. Display the target page (see Switching between pages on p. 32).

3. Drag (or **Ctrl**-drag to copy) the object from the pasteboard onto the target page.

WebPlus makes it easy to see exactly what you're working on—from a wide view of a whole page to a close up view of a small region. For example, you can use the **scroll bars** at the right and bottom of the main window to move the page and pasteboard with respect to the main window. The view automatically re-centers itself as you drag objects to the edge of the screen.

The **View toolbar** at the top of the screen provides the 🖐 **Pan Tool** as an alternative way of moving around, plus a number of buttons that let you zoom in and out so you can inspect and/or edit the page at different levels of detail.

> 💡 If you're using a wheel mouse, spinning the wheel scrolls vertically. **Shift**-spin to scroll horizontally and **Ctrl**-spin to zoom in or out!

Switching between pages

WebPlus provides a variety of ways of getting quickly to the part of your site you need to work on. The Studio's Site tab provides a central "control panel" including both the **Site Structure tree**, which depicts the hierarchy of pages in your site (see Understanding site structure and navigation on p. 27), and icons for each of the site's **master pages**.

Selecting vs. viewing a page: Single-clicking a page/master page entry merely **selects** the page. To actually **view** the associated page/master page you need to **double-click** an entry.

An orange entry (with bolded page name) denotes the selected page.

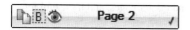

The eye icon denotes the currently viewed page—which you're able to edit in the workspace. This example shows that the page is currently in view as well as selected. It also now uses a different Master Page (B instead of A).

A highlighted master page icon in the Site tab's upper window denotes the selected master page.

Master A

An eye icon in the master page icon denotes the currently viewed page. This example shows a viewed (but unselected) master page.

To view a specific page/master page:

Several methods can be used to view a page:

- On the Hintline, use the Hintline's ◀ ▶ page navigation buttons. OR
  Click the entry for the page or master page in the **Page Locator** list.

- On the Studio's **Site** tab, double-click the entry for the page (or master page) you want to view. The Site Structure window of the tab includes a tree with entries for pages in the site, while the Master Pages window shows only master pages as thumbnails. You may need to click the **Master Pages>** button to display the master pages window.

- Click the 📇 **Site Structure** button on the Hintline or on the Site tab's Page window. Select the page entry in the dialog's tree (double-click tree entries if necessary to expand each branch). Then click the **View Page** button.

For master pages:

- On the Studio's **Site** tab, click the **Master Pages>** button to reveal a master page window. One or more master page icons will be displayed.

- Double-click the icon for the master page you want to view.

To switch between the current page and master page:

- Click the 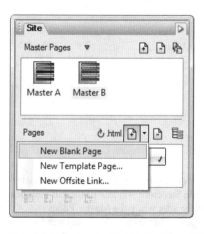 **Page/Master Page** button on the Hintline.

As a shortcut to view the site's Home page:

- Click the **Home Page** button on the Hintline.

Adding, removing, and rearranging pages

Using the Studio's Site tab, you can quickly add or delete pages at any level of your site structure, and use drag-and-drop to rearrange pages within the structure as needed, add new master pages, reassign pages to particular master pages, and add offsite links.

Use the upper Master Pages window of the Site tab to access master pages, and the Pages window (tab's central Site Structure tree) to access pages. Pages (with page content or blank) can also be added from multi-page templates (see p. 18).

Besides the Site tab, WebPlus offers a variety of other ways to manipulate pages: the **Site Structure** dialog, the **Master Page Manager**, and both standard and right-click (context) menus.

To add a new blank page:

1. Click the down arrow on the **Add** button directly above the Site tab's Pages window. From the drop-down menu, choose **New Blank Page**.

2. In the New Page Properties dialog, specify options for the new page in the Appearance tab (see Setting page properties on p. 57) as well as options only available via this dialog:

    • Duplicate the design elements from an existing web page. Check **Copy objects from page** and select the page in the activated list.
    • Specify the position of the new page in the Site Structure. In the Placement section, insert the page Before, After, or make it a Child of the named page.

3. Click **OK**.

A new page appears at the specified location in the site structure. The page uses Site Properties (p. 54) for its dimensions. You can always move the page to a different position or level, or switch to a different master page (see Rearranging pages or Assigning master pages on p. 38 and 39).

While adding standard pages lets you start page design from scratch, you can make life a little easier by adopting "ready to go" pages from supplied WebPlus templates. To maintain the page's original design, any master page associated with the added page can optionally be "imported" with the page.

To add a new page from a template:

1. In the Pages Window (Site Structure tree) of the Studio's Site tab, select a page after which you want to add the new page.

2. Click the down arrow on the **Add** button directly above the Pages window. From the drop-down menu choose **New Template Page....**

3. From the **Add New Page from Template...** dialog, select a template from the left-hand pane, and check the page for addition (check further pages for inclusion if needed).

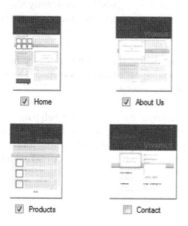

4. WebPlus lets you control if an associated master page is copied with the page. Pick from the top-left drop-down menu choosing one of:

- **Copy Master Page**. To always copy the master page into your site.

- **Compare and Copy Master Page**. Checks if the master page already exists in your site then copies it if not present.

- **No Master Page**. The page's master page is never copied to the site.

5. Click the **Open** button. The pages are added to the Site tab.

You can also add an **offsite link** to your site structure. Typically, this would be a page or resource separate from your site that you wanted to include in your site's navigation structure. The offsite link appears in the Site Structure tree and in navigation bars, so you can manipulate it just as if it were a page in your site.

To add an offsite link:

1. In the Pages Window (Site Structure tree) of the Studio's Site tab, select a page after which you want to add the new page.

2. Click the down arrow on the ⊞ ▾ **Add** button directly above the Pages window. From the drop-down menu, choose **New Offsite Link...**.

3. In the dialog, type a **Menu name** to identify the offsite link in the Site Structure tree (the equivalent of its page name).

4. Click to select the link destination type, and enter the specific offsite hyperlink target (see Selecting a hyperlink target on p. 223), and the window in which you want the target to appear. Keep **Include in Navigation** checked if the link is to appear in site-wide navigation.

    •   Check **Before** and/or **After** to apply horizontal separator lines above/below the page as a submenu item in navigation bars.

    •   Add a **Description** to add extra page-related text information on the bar's submenu item.

5. Click **OK**.

To add a new master page:

1. On the Studio's Site tab, ensure the **Master Pages>** button is clicked to expand the Master Page Window.

2. Click the ⊞ **Add** button above the Master Pages window.

A new master page appears in the Site tab's Master Pages window.

To easily distinguish between multiple master pages, you can assign them distinct names. The master pages will still adopt a letter designation as a suffix, e.g. A, B, C, etc. so you can check master page assignment in your Site Structure.

To name a master page:

1. Right-click the master page thumbnail and choose **Properties...**.

2. Edit the **Name** of the page.

To clone a page:

- In the Studio's Site tab, right-click on a selected page and choose **Clone Page**. An identical copy is inserted below the selected page.

To delete a page or master page:

1. On the Studio's Site tab, select the page (or master page) to delete by clicking its entry.

2. Click the ⬜ **Remove** button above the appropriate window to delete the page.

When you delete a page, you'll have the option to **remove** any hyperlinks in your site that point to it, or **redirect** the hyperlinks to another specified page (hyperlinks to anchors on the deleted page can optionally be deleted).

Rearranging pages

Besides using the Site Structure tree to add or delete pages, you can use it to rearrange pages as needed. Using the parent/child structure, rearranging pages is an intuitive process whether you use drag-and-drop or convenient buttons. You can move a page:

- To a different sequential position (up or down) at the same level of the structure

- To a higher (parent) level

- To a lower (child) level

To move a page:

1. Display the Studio's Site tab.

2. Single-click to select the page in the Site Structure tree.

3. (Using drag-and-drop) Drag the page entry up or down and drop it at a new position in the tree. Watch the cursor for feedback on the new position relative to that of the page just below the cursor:

   moves the page to the same level as, and following, the highlighted target page.

   makes the page a child of the highlighted target page.

Assigning individual master pages

If you've defined more than one master page for your site, you can use a variety of methods to reassign a specific master page to individual pages, one page at a time. (For an overview, see Understanding pages and master pages on p. 29.)

To assign an individual master page to a page:

- On the Studio's **Site** tab, click on the master page thumbnail (in the Master Pages section) and drag onto the page entry (in the tab's Site Structure section).

Assigning multiple master pages

For pages with more design diversity, you can assign more than one master page to each web page by using the Master Pages tab. As an example, you have two designs existing on two separate master pages—"Master **A**" and "Master **B**." Using the Master Pages tab, you can place "Master B," containing the IPSUM text, in front of the selected page, with Master A used as the page background.

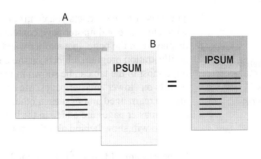

★ You'll need to create multiple master pages in advance of using the Master Pages tab.

To assign multiple master pages to a web page:

1. From the Site tab, select the page which will have multiple master pages.

2. In the Master Pages tab, click the **Add** button.

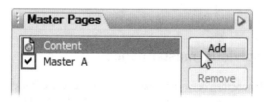

3. From the dialog's drop-down menu, select the additional already created master page, and click **OK**. Your additional master page is added to the tab (below) and the web page will be using the page elements of the newly assigned master page.

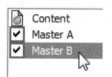

The Site tab's Site Structure shows a web page with a plus sign if multiple master pages are assigned (instead of A, B, C, etc.).

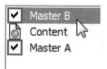

The Master Pages tab lets you control the order in which the page and master page contents are displayed on the page. In a similar way to layers in an illustration program, objects on the entry uppermost in the tab can be shown in front of objects on "lower" master pages. Master pages can also be rearranged amongst each other. Newly added master pages are added to the bottom of the stack so will show behind all other content.

In the example, Master B is positioned above all other content.

To reorder the page content and master pages:

- Select the entry in the tab and click the **Up** or **Down** button.

> To temporarily hide a master page, uncheck its entry in the tab.

To unassign a master page:

- Select the entry in the tab and click the **Remove** button.

Adding navigation bars

In WebPlus, **navigation bars** are programmed to understand your site structure, making it easy to design a site that's simple to navigate.

Navigation bars facilitate movement between the various sections and levels of a site. For example, in the navigation bar examples below, the buttons provide links to the Home page and various top-level section pages, while popup menus link to child pages (Story 1 and Story 2) within each section.

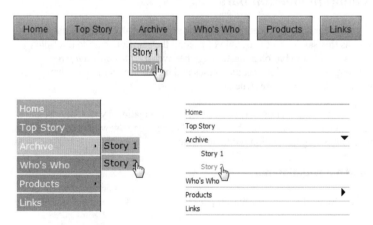

You can easily install navigation bars at any level of your site, reconfigure them to link to a particular part of the site, change the appearance of the navigation bar, and exclude particular pages from navigation as needed.

Navigation types

WebPlus offers various types of navigation bars depending on the level of functionality and design you're looking for in your navigation bar. All navigation bars are JavaScript-based, and belong to three types:

Navigation bar types	Use for:
Basic (JavaScript)	Text-based[1] navigation bars without backgrounds.
Designer (JavaScript)	Text-based[1] navigation bars with button and bar backgrounds.
Miscellaneous (JavaScript)	Combo box, vertical site map, folding style, or concertina (sliding image) navigation bars.

[1] Created as searchable HTML text.

Creating navigation bars

Navigation bars can be added to any page but are typically added to the master page—as this saves you the trouble of pasting the same element to multiple pages. A navigation bar on a master page behaves *as if it's on each page*— consistent with the notion that its buttons and menus are relative to where each page sits in the overall site structure.

When adding a navigation bar, you can choose navigation Type, Options, and a set Style. Once added, the bar can be edited at any time. New bars can be created from any existing navigation bar in your site.

To add a navigation bar:

1. Select the page (or master page).

2. Click **Insert Navigation Bar** on the **Web Objects** toolbar.

3. From the dialog's **Type** tab, a default gallery of navigation bars appears. For a different navigation type, select from the upper-right **Type** drop-down menu.

The Navigation bar gallery lets you select a navigation bar of that type, e.g.

4. From the **Navigation Type** tab choose whether to base your navigation bar directly on the site's Site Structure (enable **Based on site structure**) or customize the navigation bar's options (enable **Custom**; see Customizing navigation bars on p. 44).

   For the former method:

   • Select which buttons should be included in the navigation bar: **Top Level**, **Parent Level**, **Same Level**, **Child Level**, **Home**, **Previous and Next**, **Previous**, **Next**, **Up**, **Breadcrumb**, **Anchors**, or **Back**.
   • Depending on the main selection, you can opt to include the **child page, anchors, home page, parent page,** and/or **Hide current page**.
   • Check **Don't use page names** to use custom button names (otherwise buttons will have functional names like "Previous" or "Home").
   • Set **Target Frame/Window** to change where the new page will open. Choose from **Same Window** (most common), **New Window** (useful for off-site pages), **Top of Current Window**, **Parent Frame**, **Named Window** and **Document Frame**.

5. From the Options tab you can control how the navigation bar functions. You can change alignment and pop-up/menu positioning options.

6. (Optional) From the Style tab, you can select different coordinated menu and submenu's object and text properties.

7. Click **OK**. The navigation bar appears on your page.

When including anchors in navigation bars, you'll be able to navigate between various sections of long pages or to repeating areas as menu options.

At any time the navigation bar can be edited, either to adjust the navigation type, its options or style.

To edit a navigation bar:

1. Double-click the navigation bar (or right-click it and choose **Edit Navigation Bar...**).

2. Change settings available from the Navigation Type, Options, and Style tabs.

★ You can edit the chosen navigation bar but cannot change its type.

WebPlus also lets you base a new navigation bar on an existing one in your site, rather than use one from the Navigation bar gallery. This saves having to customize a navigation bar from the gallery again.

You'll need to deselect any existing navigation bar on your page first, otherwise it will be replaced by your new navigation bar design!

To create a new navigation bar from an existing navigation bar:

1. From the dialog's **Type** tab, enable **Copy Existing Navigation Bar**. The gallery updates to show the currently used navigation bars in your site.

2. Click **Select** next to the chosen navigation bar, then modify the navigation type or style as described under To add a navigation bar (see p. 42).

3. Click **OK**.

Customizing navigation bars

By default, navigation bar items will be based on your site structure. If you're looking to rearrange the order or hierarchy of your navigation bar items to be different from your Site Structure, WebPlus will allow you to customize any navigation bars by creating a **custom navigation tree**—you can also add, edit, or delete elements which will access a range of link destination types (see Adding hyperlinks and anchors on p. 223) just as in Site tab's Site Structure.

> ★ Once you're working with a custom navigation tree, the navigation bar will no longer automatically update when new pages are added to your site. If you still want this to happen, you'll have to base your bar on the site's Site Structure.

To customize a selected navigation bar:

1. Double-click the navigation bar.

2. From the Navigation Type tab, enable the **Custom** option, and ensure **New navigation tree** is enabled.

3. (Optional) Name the navigation tree in the Navigation Tree Name box.

4. Rearrange the order of the navigation bar items by drag and drop (or use the **Move Up**, **Move Down**, **Make Child** or **Make Parent** buttons).

5. Click **Add Link** to add a new link to the end of your navigation bar list. The element is assigned a link destination, a target frame or window and a title in the displayed dialog. Click **OK**.

   (Optional) Click **Reset** to revert the navigation tree back to its original structure. **Export Options...** let you control the location and naming of the JavaScript file used to display your custom navigation tree.

6. Click **OK** again. The navigation bar now uses the custom navigation tree to present menu options.

The custom Navigation tree which is saved is given a name (e.g., customnavtree-1) and is automatically stored in your site.

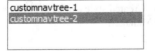

If you plan to create more navigation bars for your site, you can reuse the same custom navigation tree for your new navigation bar by selection from the dialog. Existing bars can also be swapped to use the new tree structure during editing.

Alternatively, you can use the **Copy...** button to copy the navigation tree used in a navigation bar already in your site. This will replace the current tree.

Using navigation bar styles

When you create or edit a navigation bar, you may wish to keep the bar's navigation type and structure the same, but customize its look and feel. The edited style can be overwritten or copied to a new style.

If you're working with multiple navigation bars and styles, use the Navigation Manager to swap styles between bars.

To edit a navigation bar style:

1. From the Style tab, use the flyouts and drop-down menus to create a unique style. Object colors, menu/submenu font properties, margins, spacing, and button scaling options can be set.

2. (Optional) Enter a different **Style Name**. Names are based on the original navigation bar name.

3. Click **OK**. If you didn't rename the style, the original style is overwritten using the same name. If you renamed, a new named style is created.

> ★ Check **Copy style** to make a duplicate style entry.

OR

1. Right-click the navigation bar on the page and select **Edit Style...**.

2. From the dialog, change the self-explanatory style settings..

3. (Optional) Enter a different style **Name**.

4. Click **OK**.

If you like your navigation bar style, either on creation or while editing the navigation bar, you can reuse it in the future. Created style can be applied to multiple navigation bars via the Navigation Manager.

Including/excluding pages in navigation

By default, all pages in the tree are **included in navigation**—that is, they can be linked to by navigation bars. You can **exclude** certain pages (any but the Home page) so they'll be ignored by navigation bars. For example, suppose you had a section of reference or archival pages that you didn't want visitors to explore top-down. Excluding the parent page for that section would remove it from the navigation bar. Note that excluding the page from navigation doesn't remove it from the site—the page will still appear in the Site Structure tree and you can still install hyperlinks to it; it just won't show up in a navigation bar.

To exclude a page from navigation:

- On the Studio's **Site** tab, right-click the page in the Site Structure tree and choose **Page Properties...**. Below the tree, uncheck **Include in Navigation.**

- Included pages show a ✓ mark in their page entry in the Site tab's Site Structure tree, while excluded page entries lack the mark and appear grayed out.

Using page separators in drop-down menus

For any page, offsite link, or anchor included in navigation (and appearing on a submenu), their properties can be adjusted to control separators and supporting page text within the submenu.

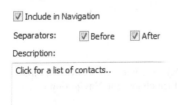

- Check **Before** and/or **After** to apply horizontal separator lines above/below the page as a submenu item in navigation bars.

- Add a **Description** to add extra page-related text information under the bar's submenu item.

Using dynamic navigation bars

Up to now, we've assumed that navigation bars are based on your site structure and show static pages as menu items. However, for more dynamic navigation bars, you can populate your navigation bar submenus with ever-changing forum and blog article titles—simply click a title to view the relevant article.

We'll assume you're using an offsite link to connect to your forum and blog, and that the offsite link is included in navigation.

To create a dynamic navigation bar:

- Right-click the offsite link in Site tab and click **Offsite Link Properties....**

- From the Offsite Link dialog, change the drop-down menu in the Smart Object Information section to add feed items (i.e., published article titles) as children to the bar's submenu.

Each article title is clickable, launching the associated article in a window, typically a separate window.

Checking your navigation bars

The **Navigation Manager** gives you an overview of all the navigation bars used in your site from within the Site Manager. (To review navigation bar basics, see Understanding site structure and navigation, p. 27)

To display the Navigation Manager:

- Click  **Site Manager** on the Default context toolbar (or Hintline at the bottom of your workspace), then choose the **Navigation** menu option.
OR

Choose **Site Manager>Navigation Manager...** from the **Tools** menu.

The **Site Manager** is launched with Navigation Manager shown by default.

The Manager displays the bar's page location, names, its navigation tree, and style, listed by page number.

To set the scope of entries displayed:

- To display links or anchors throughout the site, select **All Pages** in the Page drop-down list.

- To narrow the scope to a particular page or master page, select the page name in the first column of the main list.

To display an entry for closer inspection:

- Click to select the entry and click the **Display** button. WebPlus "zeroes in" on the selected item.

To remove a navigation bar entry:

- Click to select its entry and click the **Delete** button.

To modify a navigation bar entry:

- Click to select its entry and click the **Modify** button. A dialog appears to allow modification.

To change the navigation bar tree or style:

- For a specific navigation bar, click under its Navigation Tree or Style column and choose a new tree or style from the drop-down menu.

Using layout aids

Layout guides are visual guide lines that help you position layout elements, either "by eye" or with snapping turned on. When the snapping feature is turned on, objects you create, move, or resize will jump to align with nearby, visible layout guides. WebPlus provides a variety of layout guides to assist you: page margins, row/column guides and ruler guides.

- **Page margin** settings are fundamental to your layout, and usually are among the first choices you'll make after starting a site from scratch. Narrow margins around the perimeter are a good starting point for clean page design. The page margins are shown as a blue box which is actually four guide lines—for top, bottom, left, and right—indicating the underlying page margin settings. If you like, you can set the margins to match your current printer settings.

- **Row** and **column guides** act as an underlying layout aid, separating your page into multiple rows or columns shown with dashed blue guide lines.

- **Ruler guides** are free-floating "sticky" red guide lines that are great for aligning objects vertically or horizontally.

To define layout guides:

- Click ▦ **Layout Guides** on the Default context toolbar.

The **Margins** tab lets you set guide lines for page margins, rows, and columns. You can set the left, right, top, and bottom margins individually. The dialog also provides options for **balanced margins** (left matching right, top matching bottom).

Use the **Row and Column Guides** section to define guides for rows and columns with an optional in-between gutter (gap). If you want rows or columns of uneven width, first place them at fixed intervals, then later drag on the guides to reposition them as required.

The **Guides** tab lets you fine-position ruler guides by specifying absolute pixel positioning (guides can also be dragged onto the page from WebPlus rulers; see Creating ruler guides on p. 51).

To show or hide layout guides:

- Click or unclick **Guide Lines** on the **View** menu.

This setting also affects any ruler guides you've placed on the page area.

Creating ruler guides

WebPlus lets you to set up horizontal and vertical **ruler guides**—lines you can use to align headlines, pictures, and other layout elements, but which won't appear in your published site.

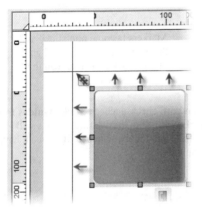

Guides are by default "sticky" so that stuck objects can be dragged around the page by their ruler guide—a great way to move previously aligned objects in bulk and simultaneously.

- To create a ruler guide, click on a ruler, hold down your mouse button, then drag onto your page. A ruler guide line appears parallel to the ruler (**Alt**-drag to create the guide at 90 degrees to the ruler).

- To move a guide, drag it.

- To remove a guide, drag and drop it anywhere outside the page area.

- To lock ruler guides, choose **Tools>Options...** and select the **Layout** option, then check **Lock guide lines**.

- For precise ruler guide placement, check **Ruler marks** in **Tools>Options>Layout** to snap guides to ruler marks.

- To unstick a selected object, click one of two small red triangular markers shown at the point where the object is attached to the guide. You'll see a link cursor (⊖) as you hover over the sticky guide marker.

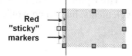

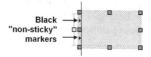

Click red marker to make non-sticky

Markers become non-sticky and change to black; object and guide are unstuck and either can then be moved.

- To turn sticky guides on and off, check/uncheck **Sticky Guides** from **Tools>Options>Layout>Layout**. Previously stuck objects will remain sticky even after sticky guides are switched off—you'll have to make them non-sticky manually.

Rulers

The WebPlus **rulers** mimic the paste-up artist's T-square, and serve several purposes:

- To act as a measuring tool.

- To create ruler guides for aligning and snapping.

- To set and display paragraph indents (see p. 91).

The actual interval size of the ruler marks depends on the current zoom percentage. In zoomed-out view, for example at 50%, there's less distance between ruler marks than when zoomed-in to 150%. To handle work where you want finer control or smaller snapping increments, click a zoom button to magnify the page.

Adjusting rulers

By default, the horizontal ruler lies along the top of the WebPlus window and the vertical ruler along the left edge. The default **ruler intersection** is the top-left corner of the pasteboard area. The default **zero point** is the top-left corner of the page area, but this can be changed.

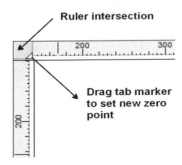

To define a new zero point:

- Drag the tab marker on the ruler intersection to the new zero point on the page or pasteboard. (Be sure to drag only the triangular marker!)

To move the rulers:

- With the **Shift** key down, drag the tab marker on the ruler intersection. Both horizontal and vertical rulers become free-floating and can then be positioned at an area on the page. The zero point remains unchanged.

- Double-click on the ruler intersection to make the rulers and zero point jump to the top left-hand corner of the page or, if selected, an object. This comes in handy for measuring objects on the page.

To restore the original ruler position and zero point:

- Double-click the tab marker on the ruler intersection.

To lock the rulers and prevent them from being moved:

- Choose **Tools>Options>Layout** and select the **Rulers** page, then check **Lock Rulers**.

Rulers as a measuring tool

The most obvious role for rulers is as a measuring tool. As you move the mouse pointer, small lines along each ruler display the current horizontal and vertical cursor position. When you click to select an object, blue ruler regions indicate the object's left, right, top, and bottom edges. Each region has a zero point relative to the object's upper left corner, so you can see the object's dimensions at a glance.

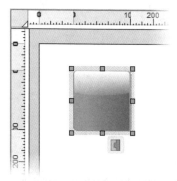

Using the dot grid

The dot grid is a matrix of dots or lines based on ruler units, covering the page and pasteboard areas. Like ruler guides, it's handy for both visual alignment and snapping.

To turn the dot grid on and off:

- Enable (or disable) the **Dot Grid** button on the **View** menu.

You can also set the grid spacing, style, and color via the Options dialog.

Setting site properties

Site properties allow settings to be made which will be applied across the entire site. Default page settings, HTML output control, search engine optimization, author/copyright, and web usage statistical information can all be set via the multi-tab Site Properties dialog. Generally speaking, decide on your Site property settings when you are planning your site—once set, the settings do not normally need to be modified (although you can at any time).

Some site properties such as page and search-engine optimization settings are also mirrored on individual pages (via Page Properties; see p. 57). This lets you override or complement the "global" Site Properties, respectively, and apply "local" settings to specific pages.

To view or change site property settings:

- Choose **Site Properties...** from the **File** menu. The Site Properties dialog appears.

The dialog is arranged into separate tabs, with each tab reflecting an aspect of site properties.

Tab	Property

Options (default) — **Default page alignment**
Lets you set a default width and height for web pages.

Default page size
Default Width and Height settings determine the dimensions of new standard web pages or master pages.

Favorites
Set an icon file (a graphic) for the site which will show when a web visitor bookmarks your website.

Default page file extension
The default extension for published pages is .HTML. Some web servers require you to use a different extension.

Warn about upper case characters in filenames
When creating new pages, the user will be warned if upper case characters are used when creating the page's file name.

Resource File Names
Controls the formatting of resource file names to allow successful upload to ISPs which impose file naming constraints.

Features — **Google Maps**
Use these options to set up Google maps (Advanced mode only).

Serif Web Resources Scheme Matching
Applies your site's color scheme to published Smart objects.

Navigation Tree
Specifies the script file used for tree control on navigation bars.

Graphics

Global image export options
Applies default format and resampling settings when exporting graphics.

HTML Output

HTML Output and Default HTML IDs
Control how your web pages are output by choosing from different encoding methods and controlling which HTML IDs are generated.

Page header
Add author details and copyright details to your site's page headers.

Publishing

Site URL
Defines the full URL address. This is a requirement for search engine optimization with sitemaps or RSS feeds.

FTP account
Sets the default FTP account used for web publishing.

FTP account settings
Displays the default FTP account settings.

Search

Search engine descriptors
Include optional descriptive information and keywords for your site.

Search Engine

Sitemaps and robots
Informs search engines or robots if they can crawl, analyze and index web pages in your site. A Sitemap file will include web pages to be indexed whereas a Robots meta tag (or a robots.txt file) controls which pages are to be excluded from indexing.

Statistics

Properties and statistics
View and change information for the current site.

Setting page size and alignment

Default site property settings for **Width** and **Height** determine the dimensions of any new page or master page. A default site property setting for **alignment** (either Left or Centered) determines how page content lines up in a browser.

One of the first things you may want to do, when creating a new site from scratch, is to check the default dimensions and adjust them if necessary. You can adjust the dimension settings at any time—but as a rule, make changes before you've gone too far with laying out page elements!

In general, use a page **Width** setting that will fit on a standard monitor (750 pixels is usually safe) and won't force users to scroll horizontally.

For page dimension and alignment, you can override the site setting for a particular page, as described in Setting page properties on p. 57.

To set the site-wide page dimension settings:

- On the dialog's **Options** tab, select different **Width** and/or **Height** values to apply to master pages.

You can also change the default page alignment setting as a site property, or override it for a given page.

To set the site-wide page alignment setting:

- On the dialog's **Options** tab, select either "Left" or "Centered" in the **Default page alignment** drop-down menu.

For more details on other tab settings, see online Help.

Setting page properties

Your WebPlus site has its own general framework, consisting of the **site** itself; one or more **master pages**; and a number of individual **pages**. Each aspect of the framework has various **property** settings that contribute to the look and behavior or your site when it's published. Whether you start with a WebPlus template or from scratch, you can choose whether to stick with the default property settings or alter them to suit your needs.

Page properties of individual pages can be viewed either via the Site tab, by right-clicking on the active page in your workspace, or via the Site Manager.

The Site Manager offers a more powerful method of not just viewing but modifying the properties of multiple pages at the same time—simply check your chosen pages and alter one or more page properties. All checked pages will adopt the new settings.

To view master page property settings:

- Click the **Master Page Manager** button above the Master Pages window on the Site tab. The Master Page Manager appears.

To view normal web page property settings:

- Right-click the page in the workspace and choose **Page Properties....**

The Page Properties dialog appears.

Tab name	Property
Navigation (default)	**Page, title, and file name** Each page has a "visible" page name or file name shown in Site tab's Site Structure tree. You can edit either, as well as choose a title different from the page name.
	Include in navigation By default, all pages are included in navigation bars. Use this option to exclude the page from navigation.
	Separators and Description If included in navigation, check **Before** and/or **After** to apply horizontal separator lines above/below the page as a submenu item in navigation bars. A **Description** box adds extra page-related text information under the bar's submenu item.
	Redirect After a configurable time interval a web page is redirected to a new hyperlink destination (another page, image, email, etc.).
Appearance	**Page alignment** Alignment determines how the page content appears in a browser. Use the Site's default page alignment setting (Use Site setting), or choose Left or Centered as an override.

Width and Height
Each master page **always** determines the size of pages that use it. For individual pages that don't use a master page you can set custom page dimensions. For pages using a master page, only the Height can be changed for the page. In the Master Page Manager (Properties button), you can override the site setting for a given master page.

Background **Master pages**
Assign one or more master pages to a specific page, or set a page to use no master page.

Use Color Scheme Designer Settings
Adopts the site's current color scheme settings for background colors or uses a custom **On-Page** color and/or **Background** color/image.

Effects **Page Entry/Exit Transitions**
Page entry and exit transitions can be applied as you navigate from one web page to another.

Use Sound file
Choose a **background** sound to load and play automatically when a specific page is first displayed.

Page Security **Page Security**
Apply access control to your web page(s) by assigning the page to a user group (via Serif Web Resources User List Smart object).

Search **Search engine descriptors**
Include optional descriptive information and keywords on individual pages, which override the site's search engine settings.

Search Engine **Sitemaps and robots**
Informs search engines or robots if they can crawl, analyze and index the current page. A Sitemap file will include the current page in indexing whereas a Robots meta tag (or a robots.txt file) will exclude the page. These settings override the site's search engine settings.

Using Site Manager

WebPlus's **Site Manager** hosts a whole range of useful site-wide information available from a single menu-driven dialog. The tool lets you view Page/Master Page Properties, and pick from a selection of Management tools for viewing and editing hyperlinks (see below), resources, text, fonts, and much more.

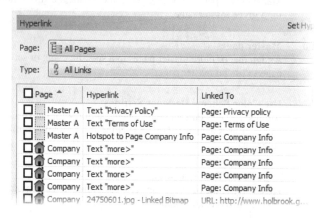

Powerful features of Site Manager include:

- The ability to control the scope and to manage an individual, a selection or all pages in your site equally.

- Any column can be sorted up or down which offers a quick way of reordering information.

- Find and Replace. Where available, this is a powerful way of applying text changes across all web pages simultaneously.

While most management tools are beneficial at any point in site development, the management of resources and text, as well as use of the Site Checker, are essential for checking your site just prior to web publishing.

To launch Site Manager:

- Click 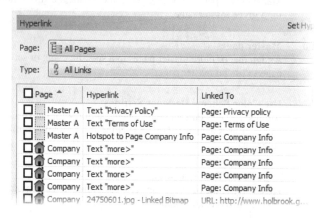 **Site Manager** on the Hintline at the bottom of your workspace (or on the Pages context toolbar).

A quick summary gives an indication of what each management feature can do for you.

Type of Management	Lets you...
Page/Master Page Properties	Include pages in navigation (with separator control), assign master pages, set page alignment and size, rename pages, set a background, add sounds, optimize pages for search engines, and apply redirections, transitions, or access control.
Hyperlink	View and edit hyperlinks, jump to hyperlinks on the page, find and replace destination links.
Anchor	View and edit anchor name and location, include pages in navigation (with separator control), jump to anchors.
Navigation	Display the navigation bars used throughout your site.
Resource	View images, media, links, HTML code resources, scripts, or applets in your site. Jump to each resource on the page, swap between linked/embedded image status, replace or resample images.
E-Commerce	View E-Commerce objects on pages across your site.
Text	View and edit text (in WritePlus), name stories, reformat text, apply styles, convert creative frames and tables to HTML-compatible text.
Font	View fonts and their availability, jump to fonts on the page, and substitute fonts.
File	Display the site structure with page file names rather than page names. Add files to your site. Rename and move file locations.
Site checker	Display common layout problems discovered in your site.

Search engine optimization

Indexing involves the automatic collection of information about your web pages by search engines such as Google, Yahoo!, Live Search, and many more. By "harvesting" this information at the search engine, search engine users can make use of this indexed information to obtain quick and accurate site search results which match the search criteria entered by the user.

By default, the contents of each published web page (especially heading text) will be indexed. However, in an Internet world of billions of web pages all being constantly indexed, web developers can optimize this indexing process to allow a site's pages to appear higher in a user's search results.

Optimization of web pages for search engines is possible in several ways:

- **Meta Tags**: Tags store **search engine descriptors** (i.e., keywords and a description) for the site and/or an individual page. These tags are used to allow better matching between entered search engine text (like you might enter into Google) and the keywords you've associated with your site or page. Additionally, a **robots meta tag** also lets you include/exclude the site or pages from being indexed; hyperlinks to other pages can also be prevented from being explored (crawled by "spiders)".

- **Robots**: Pages (or folders) can be **excluded** from search-engine indexing by using a robots file. This works in an equivalent way to the robots meta tag but uses a text file (robots.txt) to instruct robots or spiders what **not** to index. The file simply lists excluded site page/folder references.

- **Sitemaps**: The opposite of the "robots" concept; pages can be **included** to aid and optimize intelligent crawling/indexing. site page references are stored in a dedicated sitemap file (sitemap.xml).

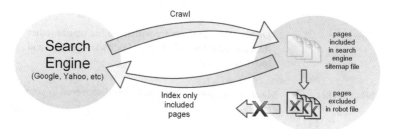

Whether you are using Meta tags, robots, or sitemaps independently or in combination, WebPlus makes configuration simple. As these settings can be established or modified for the whole site (Site Properties; Search Engine tab) any newly created page will adopt site's search engine settings. If you change the site settings, all web pages will update to the new settings automatically. However, you can override the site's settings on a specific web page (Page Properties; Search Engine tab) at any time. The page's override means that subsequent changes to site settings will always be ignored.

Using search engine descriptor Meta Tags

Although they're optional, if you want to increase the likelihood that your website will be "noticed" by major web search services, you should enter Meta Tag **search engine descriptors**. Search services maintain catalogues of web pages, often compiled through the use of "crawlers" or other programs that prowl the web collecting data on sites and their content. By including descriptive information and keywords, you'll assist these engines in properly categorizing your site. You can enter descriptors for the site as a whole and/or for individual pages. For example, for a simple ornithological site you could have the following descriptors, reflecting the content of your site or page, e.g.

	Site Properties	Page Properties
Description	American Birds Web	Egret and Heron species page
Keywords	Birds, America, Audubon	Cattle Egret, Blue Heron, Green-backed Heron

It's a good idea to plan which descriptors are used for the site and pages. If set, a site's descriptors will complement page-specific descriptors.

To enter search engine descriptors:

1. (For the site) Choose **Site Properties...** from the **File** menu.
    OR
    (For a page) Right-click the page in the workspace or Site tab and choose **Page Properties...** (or choose the item from the **Edit** menu).

2. Click the dialog's **Search** tab.

3. In the top window, type in a brief description of your site. Although the description can be any length, the first ten words or so are the most important.

4. In the next window, enter any number of keywords (separated by commas) that you think fairly categorize your site. Put yourself in the place of a potential visitor. What keywords might they enter if they were searching for exactly what your site or page has to offer?

5. Set a language code for your site from the drop-down menu to identify your site's language use. Most user's Internet search engines will permit language specific searches for web pages, so your site will show in search results according to its language code setting.

Excluding pages from indexing (robots meta tags)

A robots meta tag can be used by search engine robots to control how they access the site or page. The whole site (and pages) can be set to be indexed/not indexed, page hyperlinks followed/not followed, or any combination thereof. Site-wide settings are made by checking **Index pages on this site** and **Follow links from pages** or as overrides on specific page properties.

To enable robot Meta Tag generation:

1. (For the site) Choose **Site Properties...** from the **File** menu.
   OR
   (For a page) Right-click the page in the workspace or Site tab and choose **Page Properties...** (or choose the item from the **Edit** menu).

2. Select the Search Engine tab and check the **Create robots meta tags** option (for a page you'll need to override site-wide settings).

3. (For the site) Use the two suboptions to allow or prevent search engines indexing the entire site (check/uncheck **Index pages on this site** option) or to allow or prevent indexing of all pages linked from an indexed page (check/uncheck **Follow links from pages** option).
   OR
   (For the page) Check **Override site search engine settings** and **Create robots meta tag**, then check/uncheck the equivalent suboptions for the specific page.

Excluding pages from indexing (Robots file)

The objective of this method is the same as that for using a robots meta tag, but instead a robots.txt file is created and no robots meta tag is included in web pages. The robots.txt file is stored in the web site's root folder and can be viewed in any text editor to verify the excluded pages and folders.

To enable a robots.txt file:

1. Choose **Site Properties...** from the **File** menu.

2. From the Search Engine tab, check the **Create search engine robots file** option.

3. (For the site) To allow or prevent search engines indexing the entire site (check/uncheck **Index pages on this site** option).
    OR
    (For a page) From page properties, to prevent search engines indexing the page, check **Override site search engine settings**, then uncheck the **Index this page** option.

Including pages in indexing

So far we've looked primarily at methods of excluding web pages from indexing. Without these controls, web pages will be indexed by discovering page hyperlinks and crawling through them, harvesting keywords, descriptions, and page text to be indexed. However, this process may not be efficient as there may be a limited number of inter-page hyperlinks present throughout your site. As a result, a search engine sitemap file (sitemap.xml) can be created to act as a local lookup for crawlers to begin investigating your site. The file simply lists pages in your site that you've decided can be indexed. The file also indicates to search engines when pages have been modified, informs when the search engine should check the page and how "important" pages are in relation to each other.

The Sitemap method is especially good for "advertising" your site pages—with a greater likelihood of your pages appearing high in a user's search results.

Just like the robots file, the setting of site and page properties creates the sitemap file (this is published with your site); the file is stored in the root web folder (perhaps alongside a robots.txt file).

One requirement of using search engine sitemaps is the need to declare an absolute URL. This allows the proper URL address (e.g., **www.gizoo.com**) to be indexed, allowing search engine users to link through to your site from their search results.

To enable search engine sitemaps:

1. Choose **Site Properties...** from the **File** menu.

2. Check the **Create search engine sitemap file** option.

3. (Optional) When the above option is checked, the default sitemap.xml file can be renamed. Click the **Change...** button and edit accordingly.

4. (For the site) To populate the sitemap file with a list of all the site's web pages (for improved page "discovery"), the **Index pages on this site** option is checked. Uncheck to create an empty sitemap.xml file. OR
    (For a page) From page properties, to add the page to the sitemap file, check **Override site search engine settings**, then check the **Index this page** option. This assumes the site as a whole has not been listed in the sitemap.xml file.

5. Check/uncheck Sitemap settings including:

    *   Page's last modified date and time.

    *   Page change frequency (set drop-down menu to hourly, daily, weekly, monthly, yearly, or never): This suggests to the search engine how frequently the page is likely to change. The search engine will decide how often to index the page on the basis of this setting.

    *   Page priority rating: 0.0 (lowest) to 1.0 (highest). Sets a page priority relative to your other web pages by which search engines are most likely to index. The default can be set on site properties with specific page overrides setting a priority higher or lower than the default.

Prioritizing text with Heading HTML tags

It is possible to assign paragraphs (or text styles) in your HTML frame or HTML table with a preferred HTML tags (H1, H2 ... to H6) for export. The tags can be assigned from **Paragraph...** on the **Text** menu (choose the Paragraph>HTML option); simply pick a preferred HTML tag for your paragraph from the drop-down menu. An advantage of this is that paragraphs assigned such tags take priority over other "body" tags (e.g., those using the <P> tag) when appearing in search engine results (the H1 tag is the highest priority).

Using the Gallery

The **Gallery tab** serves as a container for storing your own design objects you'd like to reuse in the same or different websites. Once you've copied a design to the Gallery, it becomes available to any site—simply open the Gallery!

Additionally, the tab includes categorized pre-designed elements that you can customize and use as a starting point for your own designs.

The Gallery has two parts: an upper **Categories** drop-down menu and a lower **Designs** window showing a list of thumbnails representing the designs in the selected category. You can adopt a design by dragging the thumbnail onto the page.

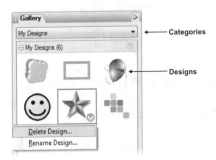

The Gallery tab can store your own designs in the ready-to-go **My Designs** category—the design is made available in any WebPlus site. When you first install WebPlus, the My Designs gallery will be empty, ready for custom designs to be added to it. New categories can be created at any time.

To further arrange your designs into logical groupings, you can add sub-categories to My Designs or to any other custom or pre-defined category.

★ Designs can be added to any pre-supplied category; the My Designs category exists simply for ease of use when storing your own custom designs.

To use a design from the Gallery:

- Click its thumbnail in the design category and drag it out onto the page. The Gallery retains a copy of the design until you expressly delete it.

To view your Gallery:

1. Click the Studio's **Gallery** tab.

2. Select a category from the drop-down menu. The items from the first listed subcategory are displayed by default.

To add, delete, or rename custom categories:

1. With the Gallery tab selected, click the ▷ **Tab Menu** button and choose **Add category...**, **Delete category**, or **Rename category...** from the flyout menu.

2. Use the dialog to enter and/or confirm your change.

If adding a category, you need to name the category in a dialog. For renaming or deletion, simply pick the category in advance of picking the option.

⚠ All designs in a deleted category will also be lost.

To add, delete, or rename custom sub categories:

- To add, select a category and click **Add Sub Category...** from the tab's ▷ **Tab Menu** button.

- To delete or rename, select options from the ⊘ drop-down button on the sub category title bar.

To move or copy an object into the Gallery:

1. Using the Categories drop-down menu, select a category into which you want to add the object. Scroll to reveal target sub-categories, expanding them if necessary.

2. Drag the object from the page and drop it onto the target category or sub-category design window (drag onto an empty sub-categories title bar to add). To copy, press the **Ctrl** key before starting to drag. A thumbnail of the design appears in the Designs window.

To rename or delete a custom design from the Gallery:

*   Click on the  drop-down button in the bottom-right corner of a thumbnail (shown by hover over) and choose from the menu.

Adding Google maps

Use embedded **Google Maps** in your web page if want to make sure that a client can locate your headquarters, attendees can find that special meeting (or event), or identify special interest locations. By embedding in a purposely designed "Directions" web page, you'll be able to add the map and written supporting directions to your site accordingly.

Each map will allow up to 10 **markers** to be placed on the map to identify each location.

A more advanced Map feature is also available for more complex mapping requirements, including an unlimited number of markers and the ability to use HTML as your marker text.

To add a simple Google map:

1. Click **Insert Google Map** on the **Web Objects** toolbar's Media flyout.

2. From the Configure Google Map dialog, enter your zip code, post code, or address in the **Search for a location** field. As Google's geolocator is being used, WebPlus will sense your locale, and display local addresses preferentially.

3. Navigate around the map using supporting panning and zoom controls—drag the hand cursor to pan, the zoom slider and buttons to magnify/zoom out. If you've got a mouse with a scroll wheel, check the **Enable mouse scroll wheel zoom** for quicker map navigation.

4. To add a marker, click **Add**, and then place the cursor over the chosen location, then click.

5. In the dialog, enter a Marker name and text for the marker, and click **OK**. The marker appears on the map preview, and its text will show when the marker is clicked. Repeat the process for each marker in turn.

6. (Optional). Enable **Show Navigation Control** buttons for either Full (panning, Zoom buttons, and Zoom slider) or Compact modes (+/- zoom in/out buttons only).

7. (Optional). Enable **Show Map Type Control** buttons for either a Bar or drop-down Menu (both showing Map, Satellite, Hybrid, and Terrain modes).

8. Click **OK**.

9. You'll see the mouse pointer change to the **Paste** cursor. What you do next determines the initial size and placement of the map.

- To insert the map at the default size, simply click the mouse.
  OR
  To set the size of the map to better fit your page design, drag out
  a region and release the mouse button.

At some point, you may want to move or delete a marker by editing the Google
map.

To edit your Google map markers:

- Double-click the Google map on your page.

- From the dialog, select a marker from the Map Markers drop-down
  list, then:

  - To edit the marker label, edit the text in the **Label** scrolling box.

  - To move the marker, click **Move**, then place the ⁻ᵢ⁻ cursor on the
    map again.

  - To delete the marker, click **Remove**.

Using Advanced Google Maps

Try the Advanced Google Maps if you've a need for greater than 10 map
markers and are interested in adding labelling and marker text that can contain
HTML code, with supporting hyperlinks and images.

You'll need to acquire a site-wide Google Maps key to enable this feature. Only
one key is allowed per site.

To enable Advanced Map mode:

1. Check **Use Advanced Maps**.

★ You'll now need to register for a Google account and then obtain a
site-wide Google API key first!

2. Click the **Go to Google Maps website** button to sign up for a key.

3.   Paste your copied key from the Google.com website into the dialog's **Google Maps key** text box.

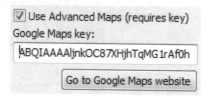

4.   To enter HTML code, type directly into the **Label** field. For more advanced coding, consider copying and pasting HTML code into the field which has been developed independently of the Google Maps dialog.

5.   Click **OK**.

To see your changes, you'll have to publish your site (see p. 291).

4 Working with Text

Importing text from a file

Importing text from a word-processor file is a quick way to build up text content for your site (but you can also create a story using WritePlus). If you use your current word processor (such as Microsoft Word) to create the text files for your site, you can import any number of files into one site.

As well as the WritePlus format (.stt), a range of popular word processing and text formats can be imported, including:

ANSI text	.txt
Microsoft Word 2007	.docx/.dotx
Microsoft Word 2000/2003	.doc/.dot
MS Works	.wps
Open Office text	.odt
Rich Text Format	.rtf
Wordperfect	.wpd
Write	.wri

For Microsoft Word formats created in any Windows operating system you don't need to have Microsoft Word installed locally. This means you can reuse third-party text content in WebPlus without the supporting application.

WebPlus will import text into either a new creative text frame (supports text flow between frames) or into a selected HTML or creative text frame (HTML frames do not support text flow) already on your web page. See Understanding text frames on p. 76 for more information.

WebPlus will preserve the formatting of imported word-processor text. However, if you're using your word processor to create text specifically for WebPlus, you'll save time by typing as text only, and applying formatting later in WebPlus.

Tables cannot be imported.

To import text from a file:

1. (Optional) If using an existing empty text frame, select the frame. If inserting text into a populated text frame, click for an insertion point (or select a portion of text to be replaced).

2. Choose **Text File...** from the **Insert** menu.

3. From the **Open** dialog, select the format of the source file to be imported and locate the file itself.

4. Check the **Retain Format** box to retain the source file's formatting styles. Uncheck the box to discard this information. In either case, WebPlus will preserve basic character properties like italic, bold, and underline, and paragraph properties like alignment (left, center, right, justified).

5. Check the **Ignore Line Wrapping** box to ignore returns in the source text—that is, only if the file has been saved with a carriage return at the end of every line, and you want to strip off these extra returns. Otherwise, leave the box unchecked.

6. Click **Open**.

7. The text will be imported into the pre-selected text object or a new text frame. If all of the imported text cannot fit into the active text frame you'll be prompted via dialog. You can either create extra frames to accommodate overflow text (click **Yes**) or just overflow the text into a hidden overflow area (click **No**).

Understanding text frames

Typically, text in WebPlus goes into **text frames**, which work equally well as containers for single words, standalone paragraphs, or multipage articles or chapter text. You can also use **artistic text** for standalone text with special effects, or **table text** (see Creating text-based tables on p. 107) for row-and-column displays.

What's a text frame?

A text frame is effectively a mini-page, with:

- Margins and column guides to control text flow.

- Optional preceding and following frames.

- Text and optional inline images that flow through the frame (from the previous frame and on to the next).

The text in a frame is called a **story**.

- When you move a text frame, its story text moves with it.

- When you resize a text frame, its story text reflows to the new dimensions.

Frames can be linked so that a single story continues from one frame to another. But text frames can just as easily stand alone. Thus in any site, you can create text in a single frame, spread a story over several frames, and/or include many independent frame sequences, e.g.

When you select a frame you'll see its bounding box (see Frame 1 above), indicated by a gray border line plus corner and edge handles, and (if you clicked with the Pointer Tool) a blinking insertion point in the frame's text. In this mode, you can edit the text with the Pointer Tool. (For details, see Editing text on the page on p. 88.)

HTML or Creative frames

Two types of frame can be added to the WebPlus page—the HTML text frame and the Creative text frame. They can be compared easily in the following table.

	HTML frames	Creative frames
Searchable by search engines (Google, etc.)	✓	✗
Script insertion for generating dynamic content	✓	✗
Margins and column guides	✗	✓
Breaks (column, page, and frame)	✗	✓
Resize/move frame	✓	✓
Crop frame	✗	✓
Rotate frame	✗	✓[1]
Frame linking	✗	✓
Columns	✗	✓
Attach objects	✓	✓
Export as text	✓	✓[2]
Copy and paste exported text	✓	✓
Solid fill and line color	✓	✓
Gradient and bitmap fill	✗	✓

HTML-compliant Styles	✓	✗
Transparency	✗	✓[1]
Borders	✗	✓[1]
Warp	✗	✓[1]
2D/3D Filter Effects	✗	✓[1]
Instant 3D	✗	✓[1]

[1] If applied, will export frame as a graphic.
[2] Only if rotate, crop, transparency, a border or a filter effect is not applied.

The above table relates to the frame as an object, and not to text contained within. For text related information, see Setting text properties on p. 97.

So how do you tell the difference between an HTML and Creative frame? Simply, HTML frames will always possess dark blue corner/edge handles when selected, while a Creative frame's handles will show as gray.

Creating frames

You add frames to a page as you would any other object. You can select, move, and resize any frame, but you cannot alter its basic shape.

To create a frame:

1. Click either the ▦ **HTML Frame Tool** or the ▦ **Creative Frame Tool** button from the Text Frames flyout on the **Standard Objects** toolbar.

2. Click on the page or pasteboard to create a new frame at a default size.
    OR
    Drag out to place the text frame at your chosen dimensions.

To delete a frame:

- Select the frame and press the **Delete** key. (If there's a selection point in the text, pressing **Delete** will remove characters after the cursor.)

You can select, move, and resize text frames just like other objects. (See p. 117, 121, and 122, respectively.)

Putting text into a frame

You can put text into an HTML or Creative frame in one of several ways. For HTML frames, text will be converted to compliant HTML code.

WritePlus story editor:	With a selected frame, click 📝 **WritePlus** on the Frame context toolbar.
Importing text:	Right-click on a frame and choose **Text File...** (shortcut **Ctrl+T**) to import text.
Typing into the frame:	Select the Pointer Tool, then click for an insertion point to type text straight into a frame, or edit existing text. (See Editing text on the page on p. 88.)
Pasting via the Clipboard:	At an insertion point in the text, press **Ctrl+V**.
Drag and drop:	Select text (e.g., in a word processor file), then drag it onto the WebPlus page. If you drop onto a selected frame, the text is pasted inline after existing text. Otherwise, a new frame is created for the text.

Creative frame setup and layout

The **frame layout** of a Creative frame controls how text will flow in the frame. The frame can contain multiple **columns**. When a frame is selected, its column margins appear as dashed gray guide lines when values for column blinds and margins are defined. Note that unlike the page margin and row/column guides, which serve as layout guides for placing page elements, the frame column guides actually determine how text flows within each frame. Text won't flow outside the column margins.

You can drag the column guides or use a dialog to adjust the top and bottom
column blinds and the left and right **column margins**.

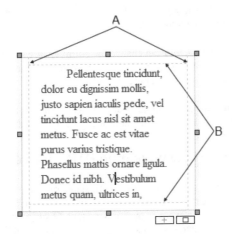

(A) Column Guides; (B) Margin Blinds

To edit frame properties directly:

- Select the frame, then drag column guide lines to adjust the boundaries
  of the column.

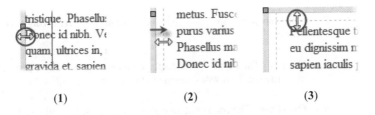

The illustration above shows how the cursor will change when hovering over the
bounding box with **Ctrl** key pressed (**1**), after dragging inwards the column
margin can be adjusted (**2**), and after dragging downwards, the top margin blind
can be moved (**3**).

To edit frame properties using a dialog:

1. Select the Creative frame and click the **Frame Setup** button on the Frame context toolbar.

2. From the dialog, you can change the **Number of columns**, **Gap** distance between columns, **Left Margin**, **Right Margin**, and enable/disable text wrapping around an object.

3. To change the column widths and blinds (top and bottom frame margins), click a cell in the table and enter a new value.

Controlling overflowing text (in HTML frames)

As HTML frames have to comply with HTML standards, they are not capable of linking stories (as for Creative frames). As a result, a decision has to be made about what happens in the event of overflowing text. Overflowing HTML frames are clearly indicated—when selected, the **Link** button at the bottom right of the frame indicates ⬚ **Overflow**.

If you see this, you can choose to leave the text **Hidden**, let it **Overflow**, or let all the text be viewable with the help of a scroll bar.

To control overflowing text:

1. Select your overflowing HTML text frame.

2. Right-click on your frame, and go to **Text Format>Overflowing text** and choose:

   - **Hidden** - The frame as it is displayed on your page will be shown in a browser. Text will continue to be hidden.

   - **Overflow** - The frame will overflow (be extended) to allow all text within the frame to be shown.

   - **Auto Scroll bar** - A navigation scroll bar is displayed only when text overflows the frame.

   - **Fixed Scroll bar** - A navigation scroll bar is displayed permanently but will be grayed out if text does not overflow.

★ It's always a good idea to preview your HTML frames (via Preview in Window or via your browser)—especially if **Overflow** is selected.

How a story flows through a sequence of Creative frames

★ Stories cannot flow between HTML frames, as they do not support linking (text can only overflow a single frame).

You can have just one Creative frame on its own, or you can have many frames. Frames can be connected in linked **sequences** so that the **story** associated with a given frame sequence flows through the first frame on to the next and keeps flowing into frames in the link sequence.

A key difference from a word processor is that WebPlus does not normally add or remove frames according to the amount of text. The text simply flows until the text runs out (and some frames are left empty), or the frames run out (and some text is left over).

- If the text runs out before the last frame, you'll have some empty frames. These frames will be filled with text if you add more text to the story, or if you increase the size of the story text.

- If there is still more text to go after filling the last frame, WebPlus stores it in an invisible **overflow area**, remembering that it's part of the story text. If you later add more frames or reduce the size of text in a frame, the rest of the story text is flowed in.

WebPlus keeps track of multiple linked frame sequences, and lets you flow several stories in the same site. The Site Manager's **Text** menu item (accessed via the **Tools** menu) provides an overview of all stories and lets you choose which one you want to edit.

On text overflow, the frame's ⌊ + ⌋ AutoFlow button can be used to create new frames for the overflowed text. To control how the frame text is spread throughout available frames, you can use **Fit Text**, **Enlarge Text**, or **Shrink Text**. These options scale a story's text size.

Using artistic text

Artistic text is standalone text you type directly onto a page. Especially useful for headlines, pull quotes, and other special-purpose text, it's easily formatted with the standard text tools.

Here are some similarities between frame text and artistic text. Both text types let you:

- vary character and paragraph properties, apply named text styles, edit text in WritePlus, and import text.

- apply different line styles, fills (including gradient and bitmap fills), and transparency.

- embed inline images.

- apply filter effects and rotate/flip.

- use proofing options such as AutoSpell/Spell Checker, Proof Reader, and Thesaurus.

- manage their content and track font usage via the Site Manager.

And some differences:

- You can initially "draw" artistic text at a desired point size, and drag it to adjust the size later. Frame text reflows in its frame upon frame resize.

- Artistic text can be applied to a path but frame text cannot.

- Artistic text won't automatically line wrap like frame text.

- Artistic text doesn't flow or link the way frame text does; the Frame context toolbar's text-fitting functions aren't applicable to artistic text.

To create artistic text:

1. Choose the **Artistic Text Tool** from the **Standard Objects** toolbar's Text flyout.

2. Set initial text properties (font, style, etc.) as needed before typing, using the Text context toolbar, **Text** menu, or right-click (choose **Text Format>**).

3. Click anywhere on the page for an insertion point using a default point size, or drag to specify a particular size as shown here.

4. Type directly on the page to create the artistic text.

Once you've created an artistic text object, you can select, move, resize, delete, and copy it just as you would with a text frame. Solid colors, gradient/bitmap fills and transparency can all be applied.

To resize or reproportion an artistic text object:

- Drag the object's handles to resize it while maintaining the object's proportions.

- To resize freely, hold down the **Shift** key while dragging.

To edit artistic text:

- Drag to select a range of text, creating a blue selection.

You can also double-click to select a word.

Now you can type new text, apply character and paragraph formatting, edit the text in WritePlus, apply proofing options, and so on.

Putting text on a path

"Ordinary" straight-line artistic text is far from ordinary—but you can extend its creative possibilities even further by flowing it along a curved path.

The resulting object has all the properties of artistic text, plus its path is a Bézier curve that you can edit with the **Pointer Tool** as easily as any other line! In addition, text on a path is editable in some unique ways, as described below.

To apply a preset curved path to text:

1. Create an artistic text object.

2. With the text selected, click the  **Path flyout** on the Text context toolbar and choose a preset path.

The text now flows along the specified path, e.g., for "Path - Top Circle."

To add artistic text along an existing line or shape:

1. Create a freehand, straight, or curved line (see Drawing and editing lines on p. 144) or a shape (see Drawing and editing shapes on p. 148).

2. Choose the **A** **Artistic Text Tool** from the **Tools** toolbar's Text flyout.

3. Bring the cursor very close to the line. When the cursor changes to include a curve, click the mouse where you want the text to begin.

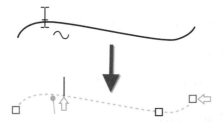

4. Begin typing at the insertion point. Text flows along the line, which has been converted to a path.

To fit existing text to an existing line or shape:

1. Create an artistic text object.

2. Create a freehand, straight, curved line or a shape.

3. Select both objects. On the **Tools** menu, choose **Fit Text to Curve**. The text now flows along the specified path.

To create text and path at the same time:

1. Choose one of the Path Text tools from the Text flyout:

     The **Freehand Path Text Tool** lets you sketch a curved line in a freeform way.

     The **Straight Path Text Tool** is for drawing a straight line.

     The **Curved Path Text Tool** lets you join a series of line segments (which may be curved or straight) using "connect the dots" mouse clicks.

2. Create a line on the page. Your line appears as a path with an insertion point at its starting end (for a curved path you can either type directly onto any part of the path or press **Esc** or double-click to get the insertion point at the start of the path).

3. Begin typing at the insertion point. Text flows along the path.

To remove the text path:

1. Select the path text object.

2. Click the ✕ ▾ **Path-None** button on the Text context toolbar's Path flyout.

The text remains as a straight-line artistic text object; the path is permanently removed.

Editing text on the page

You can use the Pointer Tool to edit frame text, table text, or artistic text directly. On the page, you can select and enter text, set paragraph indents and tab stops, change text properties, apply text styles, and use Find and Replace (see p. 92). For editing longer stories, and for more advanced options, choose WritePlus (**Edit Story...** from the **Edit** menu).

Selecting and entering text

The selection of frame text, artistic text, and table text follows the conventions of the most up-to-date word-processing tools. The selection area is shaded in semi-transparent blue for clear editing.

Nulla vestibulum eleifend
nulla. Suspendisse potenti.
Aliquam turpis nisi, venenatis
non, accumsan nec, imperdiet
laoreet, lacus.

Double-, triple-, or quadruple-click selects a word, paragraph or all text, respectively. You can also make use of the **Ctrl**-click or drag for selection of non-adjacent words, the **Shift** key for ranges of text.

To edit text on the page:

1. Select the **Pointer Tool**, then click (or drag) in the text object. A standard insertion point appears at the click position (see below).
    OR
    Select a single word, paragraph or portion of text.

2. Type to insert new text or overwrite selected text, respectively.

    Nulla |vestibulum eleifend
    nulla. Suspendisse potenti.
    Aliquam turpis nisi, venenatis
    non, accumsan nec, imperdiet
    laoreet, lacus.

To start a new paragraph:

*   Press **Enter**.

To start a new line within the same paragraph (using a "line break" or "soft return"):

*   Press **Shift+Enter**.

The following two options apply only to frame text. You can use these shortcuts or choose the items from the **Insert>Break** submenu.

To flow text to the next column (Column Break) or frame (Frame Break):

- Press **Ctrl+Enter** or press **Alt+Enter**, respectively.

To switch between insert mode and overwrite mode:

- Press the **Insert** key.

To repeat a text action:

- Choose **Repeat** from the **Edit** menu, or press **Ctrl+Y**.

For example, if you've applied new formatting to one paragraph, you can click in another paragraph and use the **Repeat** command to apply the same formatting there.

To show special characters:

- From the **View** menu, select **Special Characters** (paragraph marks and breaks; see below) or **Spaces** (Show Special Characters plus tabs, non-breaking spaces, hyphenation points, and "filled" normal spaces).

Praesent nisl tortor, laoreet eu, dapibus quis, egestas non, mauris.
 Cum sociis natoque penatibus, nascetur ridiculus mus.

Nullam eleifend pharetra felis. Mauris nibh velit, tristique lacinia in.

Praesent nisl tortor, laoreet eu, dapibus quis, egestas non, mauris.↵
 Cum sociis natoque penatibus, nascetur ridiculus mus.¶

Nullam eleifend pharetra felis. Mauris nibh velit, tristique lacinia in.§

Copying, pasting and moving text

You can easily copy and paste text using standard commands; drag and drop of text is also supported.

> ★ If you don't place an insertion point, the text can be pasted into a new text frame directly.

Setting paragraph indents

When a text object is selected, markers on the horizontal ruler indicate the left indent, first line indent, and right indent of the current paragraph. You can adjust the markers to set paragraph indents, or use a dialog.

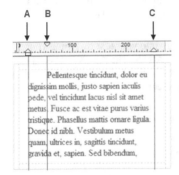

(A) Left Indent; (B) 1st Line Indent; (C) Right Indent.

- The **Left** indent is set in relation to the object's left margin.

- The **1st line** indent is in relation to the left indent.

- The **Right** indent is in relation to the object's right margin.

For details on setting frame margins, see Frame setup and layout on p. 80.

To set the indents of the current paragraph:

- Drag the appropriate ruler marker(s).
  OR

  For quick left indents, select the ⬆ **Increase Level** or ⬇
  Decrease Level button to increase or decrease indent, respectively.
  Indent is by the currently set default tab stop distance.
  OR
  To adjust indent settings via a dialog, choose **Paragraph...** from the
  Text menu (or **Text Format>Paragraph...** from the right-click
  menu). In the Indentation box, you can enter values for Left, Right, 1st
  Line, or Hanging indents.

Working with Unicode text

WebPlus fully supports **Unicode**, making it possible to incorporate foreign characters or special symbols.

- To paste Unicode text from the Clipboard to the page, use **Edit>Paste Special...,** then select "Unformatted Unicode Text."

- Insert Unicode characters directly into your text by typing your Unicode Hex value and pressing **Alt+X**. The Alt+X keyboard operation toggles between the displayed character (e.g., @) and its Hex value (e.g., U+0040) equivalent.

- To export text in Unicode format, use WritePlus.

Using Find and Replace

You can search site text for an extraordinary variety of items: not just words or parts of words, but a host of character and paragraph attributes such as fonts, styles, alignment, bullets and numbering, missing fonts, drop caps... even inline graphics and more! Using the Find and Replace dialog—which remains open without interrupting your work until you click its **Close** button—you can replace globally, or on a case-by-case basis.

To use Find and Replace:

1. Choose **Find & Replace...** from the **Edit** menu.

2. In the dialog, type the text to be found in the **Find** box and its replacement text (if any) in the **Replace** box. Click the down arrows to view recent items. Click either box's button to use flyout menus to select formats or special characters, or define a regular expression (for a wildcard-type search).

3. Select the Range to be searched: **Current Story** (just the currently selected text object or story), or **All Stories** (all text), or **Current Selection** (only used with the Replace All function to operate on the currently selected text).

4. Select **Match whole word only** to match character sequences that have **white space** (space, tab character, etc.) or punctuation at each end, or which are at the start/end of a paragraph. Select **Match case** for case-sensitive search. Select **Regular expressions** to treat the contents of the Find box as an expression, rather than as a literal string to be found.

5. Click **Find Next** to locate the next instance of the Find text.
    OR
    Click **Select All** to highlight all instances of matching text in your site simultaneously.

6. Click **Replace** if you want to substitute the replacement text. Alternatively, click **Find Next** again to skip to the next matching text. Continue using the Replace option as required until you reach the end of your site.
    OR
    Click **Replace All** to replace all instances of the Find text with the replacement text at the same time. WebPlus reports when the search is completed.

7. Click **Close** to dismiss the Find and Replace dialog.

The Find and Replace dialog also lets you perform a wildcard-type search by using a **regular expression**—a formula for generating a set of strings—to specify complex search criteria. This is covered in more detail in the WebPlus Help.

5 Formatting Text

Setting text properties

WebPlus gives you a high degree of control over the fine points of typographic layout, whether you're working with frame text, table text, or artistic text.

To apply basic text formatting:

1. Select the text.

2. Use buttons on the Text context toolbar to change text style, typeface, point size, attributes, paragraph alignment, or level.

By default, text on your published web pages is set to vary in size depending on the visitor's browser setting. If you wish, you can override this as a global option in WebPlus, so that text will appear in the browser at exactly the same point sizes used in your layouts. To check or change the setting, choose **Site Properties...** from the **File** menu. On the HTML Output tab, check **Force absolute text size** to override the variable-text default.

To clear local formatting (restore plain/default text properties):

- Select a range of text with local formatting.

- Click on the **Clear Formatting** option on the Text context toolbar's text styles drop-down list (or Text Styles tab).

Using fonts

One of the most dramatic ways to change your site's appearance is to change the fonts used in your artistic text, frame text, or table text. Applying different fonts to a character or entire paragraph can communicate very different messages to your intended readership.

Lorem Ipsum

LOREM IPSUM

Lorem Ipsum *Lorem Ipsum*

Lorem Ipsum

Font assignment is very simple in WebPlus, and can be done from the **Fonts** tab, Text context toolbar, or in the **Character** dialog (via right-click, or from the **Text** menu).

The Fonts tab lets you:

- Apply fonts easily without dialog navigation.

- Assign fonts to be Websafe or favorites.

- View most recently used, Websafe, and your favorite fonts simultaneously.

- Make a font rasterize on export or resolve its export in Site Checker.

- Search for installed fonts via search box.

- Hover-over preview of fonts applied to your site's text (optional).

- Change a font for another throughout your site (by right-click Select All).

- Access Serif FontManager (if purchased).

The Fonts tab is automatically hidden by default, but can be viewed by clicking the arrow button at the left of your workspace. You may also need to click the **Fonts** label to display the **Fonts** tab.

Websafe fonts are a specially selected and configurable subset of fonts which offer the best font matches between your site (during design) and your web visitors' computers (during browsing). On publishing, Websafe fonts are only referenced (and not rasterized) as they are assumed to be available on a web visitor's computer.

Generally speaking, it is advisable to keep to the standard list of Websafe fonts shown in the Fonts tab unless you can be sure of font usage amongst your target audience. These fonts are grouped together under the tab's Websafe category (an equivalent category exists on the text context toolbar's Font drop-down menu).

Using text styles

WebPlus lets you use named **text styles** (pre- or user-defined), which can be applied to frame text, table text, or artistic text. A text style is a set of character and/or paragraph attributes saved as a group. When you apply a style to text, you apply the whole group of attributes in just one step. For example, you could use named paragraph styles for particular layout elements, such as "Heading," "Quote," or "Body," and character styles to convey meaning, such as "Emphasis," "Code," or "Reference."

Styles can be applied to characters or paragraphs using either the Text context toolbar or the Text Styles tab. Both paragraph and character styles can be managed from the **Text Style Palette**.

The Text Styles tab also lets you create new styles from scratch, create named styles from existing text properties, and swap a style for another across your site in one operation. Any style can be previewed against any selected paragraph directly on the page. See online Help for more details on these features.

Paragraph styles and character styles

A **paragraph style** is a complete specification for the appearance of a paragraph, including all its font and paragraph format attributes. Every paragraph in WebPlus has a paragraph style associated with it.

- WebPlus includes one built-in paragraph style called **"Normal"** with a specification consisting of generic attributes including left-aligned, 12pt Verdana. You can modify the "Normal" style by redefining any of its attributes, and create or adopt any number of new or pre-defined styles having different names and attributes.

- Applying a paragraph style to text updates all the text in the paragraph except sections that have been locally formatted. For example, a single word marked as bold would remain bold when the paragraph style was updated or changed.

A **character style** includes only font attributes (name, point size, bold, italic, etc.), and you apply it at the character level—that is, to a range of selected characters—rather than to the whole paragraph.

- Typically, a character style applies emphasis (such as italics, bolding or color) to whatever underlying font the text already uses; the assumption is that you want to keep that underlying font the same. The base character style is shown in the Text Styles tab (or palette) as **"Default Paragraph Font,"** which has no specified attributes but basically means "whatever font the paragraph style already uses."

- Applying the Default Paragraph Font option from the Text Styles tab (or the Text context toolbar's Styles box) will strip any selected local character formatting you've added and will restores original text attributes (paragraph styles are not affected).

- As with paragraph styles, you can define any number of new character styles using different names and attributes (or adopt a pre-defined character style).

Working with named styles

Normal ▾ The named style of the currently selected text is displayed in either the Text Styles tab or the drop-down **Styles** box on the Text context toolbar. A character style (if one is applied locally) may be shown; otherwise it indicates the paragraph style.

To apply a named style:

1. Using the Pointer Tool, click in a paragraph (if applying a paragraph style) or select a range of text (if applying a character style). If you apply a paragraph style, it will be applied to the whole paragraph regardless of the amount of text selected. If you've selected text in more than one paragraph, the change takes place in all selected paragraphs.

2. Display the Text Styles tab and select a style from the style list.
   OR
   On the Text context toolbar, click the arrow to expand the Styles drop-down list and select a style name.

The Text Style tab highlights the paragraph or character style applied to any selected text.

As both paragraph and character formatting can be applied to the same text, all of the current text's formatting is displayed in the **Current format** box on the tab. In the example below, currently selected text has a Strong character style applied over a Normal paragraph style.

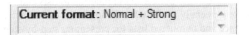

To modify an existing style:

1. From the Text Styles tab:

   - Right-click on the character or paragraph style you want to modify and then choose **Modify <style>...**.
     OR

   - With a style selected, pick the **Manage Styles** button from the Text Styles tab, then choose the **Modify...** button.

2. From the Text Style dialog, define (or change) the style name, base style, and any character or paragraph attributes, tabs, bullets, and drop caps you want to include in the style definition.

3. Click **OK** to accept style properties, or **Cancel** to abandon changes.

4. Click **Apply** to update text, or click **Close** to maintain the style in the site for future use.

Alternatively, choose **Text Style Palette...** from the **Text** menu to modify styles and to change text defaults (see p. 137).

To delete one or more text styles:

-   Right-click a text style and select **Delete <style>...**.

-   From the dialog, click **Remove**. For deletion of multiple styles, check multiple style names first. For removal of all or unused styles, use appropriate buttons.

⚠ Take care when deleting styles. Styles based on a checked "parent" style will be checked for deletion.

Creating a bulleted or numbered list

For any text frame it's possible to apply bullets and numbering to lists and paragraphs alike. Bullets are especially useful when listing items of interest in no specific order of preference and numbered lists for presenting step-by-step procedures (by number or letter). WebPlus lets you apply the list style to normal text (as local formatting) or to text styles equally.

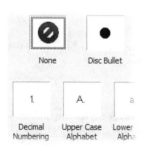

None   Disc Bullet

1.   A.   a

Decimal   Upper Case   Lower
Numbering   Alphabet   Alpha

Within HTML text frames, basic bullet icons, numbers (numeric and Roman) and letters can be applied.

However, if you're using Creative text frames you can adopt basic as well as complex **bulleted** or **numbered** lists either by selecting presets (see below) or creating your own custom list style (these let you select your own symbols, numbers and letter formats). You then have the option of replacing an existing preset with your own preset based on your custom list style.

Bulleted list

Numbered list

To create a simple bulleted or numbered list:

1. Select one or more paragraphs.
   OR
   Click in a paragraph's text.

2. Select ⦂☰ **Bulleted List** or ⦂☰ **Numbered List** from the Text context toolbar.

The list style used is the first preset shown in the Bullets & Numbering dialog described below.

To create a bulleted or numbered list (using presets):

1. Select one or more paragraphs.
   OR
   Click in a paragraph's text.

2. Select **Bullets & Numbering...** from the **Text** menu.

3. From the Text Style dialog, either:

   - For text in HTML text frames, click in a preset icon from the dialog (see above).
     OR

   - For text in Creative text frames, pick **Bullet** or **Number** from the **Style** drop-down menu, then select one of the preset formats shown by default.
     OR

   - For a custom list, select a preset then click the **Details** button to alter custom options.

4. Click **OK** to apply list formatting.

Each time you insert a following return, a new line will begin with the specified symbol or number. In addition, typing two returns in a row (pressing **Enter** twice) cancels bullets or numbers and resumes regular paragraph formatting.

> Turn off list formatting by clicking the ⁝≣ or ⁝≣ buttons on the Text context toolbar again.

To restart list numbering (Creative frame text only):

1. Click to place an insertion point in the list to set the restart position, then select **Bullets & Numbering...** from the **Text** menu.

2. From the Presets or Details page, check **Restart Numbering** to reset the number or letter sequence back to 1 or A, respectively.

3. Click **OK**.

To turn off bullets or numbering formatting:

1. Select the paragraph with list formatting.

2. Select **Text>Bullets & Numbering...** from the **Text** menu.
OR
Right-click the paragraph and from the **Text Format** option, choose **Bullets & Numbering...**.

3. In the **Text Styles** dialog, click the **None** preset option.

WebPlus also lets you assign bullets and numbers to styles. (See WebPlus help.)

6   Working with Tables

Creating text-based tables

Tables are ideal for presenting text and data in a variety of easily customizable row-and-column formats, with built-in spreadsheet capabilities.

Each cell in a table behaves like a mini-frame. Like frame text you can vary character and paragraph properties, apply named text styles, embed inline images, apply text color fills (solid, gradient, or bitmap), and use proofing options such as Spell Checker, Proof Reader, and Thesaurus. Some unique features include number formatting and formula insertion.

HTML or Creative tables

Two types of table can be applied to the WebPlus page—the HTML table and the Creative table. These can be compared easily below—some features can be applied to both, or just to one or the other.

	HTML tables	Creative tables
Searchable by search engines (Google, etc.)	✓	✗
Script insertion for generating dynamic content	✓	✗
Resize/move table	✓	✓
Crop table	✗	✗
Rotate table	✗	✓[1]
Rotate table text (in cell)	✗	✓[1]

Sort table contents	✓	✓
Solid fill and border color	✓	✓
Gradient and bitmap fill	✗	✓
HTML-compliant Styles	✓	✗
Transparency	✗	✓[1]
Borders	✗	✓[1]
Warp	✗	✓[1]
2D/3D Filter effects	✗	✓[1]
Instant 3D	✗	✓[1]
QuickClear/QuickFill/AutoFormat	✓	✓
Edit cell text in WritePlus	✓	✓
View cell text in Site Manager	✓	✓
Import of Excel and text files	✓	✓

[1] If applied, will export table as a graphic.

Rather than starting from scratch, WebPlus is supplied with a selection of pre-defined table formats, i.e. templates, that can be used. Simply pick one and fill in the cells with content.

WebPlus lets you:

- Edit the pre-defined format before adding a new table to the page.

- Create your own custom formats without creating a table. See Creating custom table formats in online Help.

- Edit existing tables to fit a different format (pre-defined or custom).

To create a table:

1. On the **Standard Objects** toolbar, choose either the 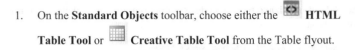 **HTML Table Tool** or ▦ **Creative Table Tool** from the Table flyout.

2. Click on the page or pasteboard, or drag to set the table's dimensions. The Create Table dialog appears with a selection of preset table formats shown in the **Format** window.

3. Step through the list to preview the layouts and select one. To begin with a plain table, select **(Default)**.

4. (Optional) Click Edit if you want to further customize your chosen format.

5. Set the **Table Size**. This is the number of rows and columns that make up the table layout.

6. Click **OK**. The new table appears on the page.

> To differentiate between table types on the page, HTML tables will always possess dark blue corner/edge handles when selected, while a Creative table's handles will show as gray.

To modify the structure and cell contents of HTML or Creative tables, please see Manipulating tables in online Help.

Inserting a calendar

The **Calendar Wizard** helps you design month-at-a-glance calendars for use on your web page.

June 2009

1	M	Holiday Leave
2	T	
3	W	Away on Business
4	T	Away on Business
5	F	
6		Anniversary
7		

The calendar is created as a scalable text-based table so you can edit text using the standard text tools. The properties of a selected calendar are similar to those of a table, and can be modified identically. Like custom table formats you can create your own custom calendar formats.

The wizard lets you set up the month/year and calendar style/format, and controls the inclusion of personal events and/or public holidays. The **Calendar Event Manager** lets you add personal events before or after adding a calendar to the page.

For calendar-specific properties, a context toolbar lets you change an existing calendar's month/year, modify calendar-specific properties, and manage calendar events (both personal and public holidays).

At any time, you can update calendar details throughout your site via **Set User Details**—in the same way that you'd set up the date (along with the time) on some alarm clocks. This is especially useful if you want to update the year on a year-to-view web page, composed of 12 monthly calendars—you only need to change the year in one place.

To insert a calendar:

1. Click the **Table** flyout on the **Standard Objects** toolbar and choose **Insert Calendar**.

2. Click again on your page, or drag out to indicate the desired size of the calendar.

3. From the displayed **Calendar Wizard**, define options for your calendar including setting the year and month, calendar style (square, or in single or multiple column format), week start day, display options, switching on personal events/holidays, and calendar format.

To have your country's public holidays shown, check **Add public holidays** in the wizard and select a **Region** from the associated drop-down menu. To add personal events, check **Add personal events** additionally.

4. Click **Finish** to complete the wizard.

To view and edit a selected calendar's properties:

1. Click the **Edit Calendar** button on the Calendar context toolbar.

2. Choose an appropriate tab (Date, Style, Events, etc.) and make your modification, then press **OK**.

Right-click (with the **Calendar** option selected) also lets you select, insert, distribute, delete, and adjust widths/heights for rows (or columns), as well as autofit to cell contents, but take care not to corrupt your table formatting!

To update calendar details globally:

1. Select **Set User Details...** from the **Tools** menu.

2. From the dialog's Calendars tab, select the **Year** that all your calendars will adopt from the drop-down menu.
   OR

3. In the Events section, check **Show public holidays** and/or **Show personal events** if all calendars are to adopt the holidays and events already configured in the Calendar Event Manager (to modify personal events, click the **Events** button).

Adding public holidays

When you create a calendar you can set up the appropriate public holidays for the country you reside in. The holidays will show up in your calendar automatically if **Add public holidays** is checked in Calendar Properties.

To enable public holidays:

1. Select your calendar's bounding box, and click **Edit Calendar** on the context toolbar.

2. From the Events tab, check **Add public holidays**.

3. (Optional) Swap to a different country's public holiday settings by using the **Region** drop-down list.

4. Click **OK**.

To display public holidays:

1. Select your calendar's bounding box.

2. Click **Calendar Events** on the context toolbar.

3. Enable the **Show public holidays** option.

Adding personal events

You can complement your public holiday listings (e.g., Easter holidays) by adding personal events such as birthdays, anniversaries, and bill payments (unfortunately!) so that the events show up on your calendar—simply use the **Calendar Events** button on a selected calendar's context toolbar. Events show automatically on your calendar under the chosen date.

To add an event:

1. Select a calendar.

2. Click **Calendar Events** on the context toolbar.

3. (Optional) Check **Show events by date** to add, edit, or delete events using a traditional calendar layout. Leave unchecked for a row-by-row Date/Event listing. If using the latter method, enable the **Show personal events** button.

4. Click 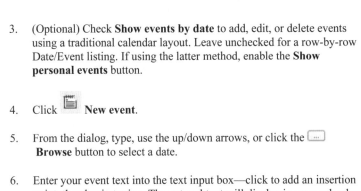 **New event**.

5. From the dialog, type, use the up/down arrows, or click the ⬚ **Browse** button to select a date.

6. Enter your event text into the text input box—click to add an insertion point, then begin typing. The entered text will display in your calendar under the chosen date.

7. If the event is a birthday or other annual event, check **Event recurs annually**.

8. Click **OK**.

9. When you have finished adding events, click the **Save** button.

    Use the 📋 **Edit Event** or ✕ **Delete Event** buttons to modify or delete an existing event.

★ Remember to ensure that **Add personal events** is checked in Calendar Properties.

7 Editing Objects

Selecting an object

Before you can change any object, you need to select it using one of these tools from the **Tools** toolbar:

 Pointer Tool
Click to use the **Pointer Tool** to select, move, copy, resize or rotate objects.

 Rotate Tool
Click to use the **Rotate Tool** to rotate an object around a rotation origin (normally centered). See Rotating an object on p. 123.

To select an object:

- Click on the object using one of the tools shown above.

  The above example shows an unselected and selected object (showing Move and Group buttons).

- If objects overlap, **Alt**-click until the desired object is selected.

When selecting a text object with the Pointer Tool:

- Clicking on a text object (artistic text or text frame) with the Pointer Tool selects the object and also positions the blinking text selection cursor within the object's text. In this mode, you can edit the text (see p. 88).

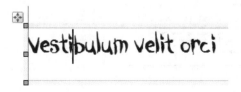

- Double-, triple-, or quadruple-click to select a word, paragraph, or all text.

- To select only the text frame, click the frame's bounding box.

- Clicking on a group selects the grouped object. **Ctrl**-click to select an individual object within a group.

Selecting multiple objects

Selecting more than one object at a time (creating a **multiple selection**) lets you:

- Position or resize all the objects at the same time.

- Create a **group object** from the multiple selection, which can then be treated as a single object, with the option of restoring the individual objects later. See Creating Groups on p. 136.

To create a multiple selection:

- Drag a "marquee" box around the objects you want to select.

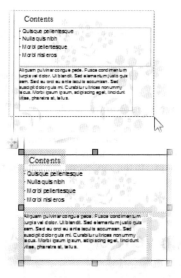

Alternatively, hold down the **Shift** key and click each object in turn.

To add or remove objects from a multiple selection:

- Hold down the **Shift** key and click the object to be added or removed.

To deselect all objects in a multiple selection:

- Click in a blank area of the page.

To select all objects on the page (or master page):

- Choose **Select All** from the **Edit** menu (or press **Ctrl+A**).

To select all objects of one type on the page (or master page):

- Hold down the **Ctrl** key and double-click one object of that type.
  OR
  Click on an object to select it and choose **Select Similar** from the **Edit** menu.

Copying, pasting, and replicating objects

Besides using the Windows Clipboard to copy and paste objects, you can duplicate objects easily using drag-and-drop, and replicate multiple copies of any object in precise formations. You can also transfer the formatting of one object to another, with the option of selecting specific attributes to be included when formatting is pasted.

To copy an object (or multiple selection) to the Windows Clipboard:

- Click **Copy** on the **Standard** toolbar.

If you're using another Windows application, you can usually copy and paste objects via the Clipboard.

To paste an object from the Clipboard:

- Click **Paste** on the **Standard** toolbar.

The standard Paste command inserts the object at the insertion point or (for a separate object) at the center of the page. To insert a separate object at the same page location as the copied item, use the **Paste in Place** command.

To choose between alternative Clipboard formats:

- Choose **Paste Special...** from the **Edit** menu.

To duplicate an object:

1. Select the object, then press the **Ctrl** key.

2. Drag the object via the 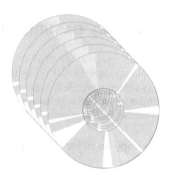 **Move** button to a new location on the page, then release the mouse button.

3. To constrain the position of the copy (to same horizontal or vertical), press and hold down the **Shift** key while dragging. A duplicate of the object appears at the new location.

Replicating objects

Duplicating an object means making just one copy at a time. The **Replicate** command lets you create multiple copies in a single step, with precise control over how the copies are arranged, either as a linear series or a grid. You can include one or more transformations to produce an interesting array of rotated and/or resized objects. It's great for repeating backgrounds, or for perfectly-aligned montages of an image or object.

To replicate an object:

1. Select the object to be replicated and choose **Replicate...** from the **Edit** menu. The Replicate dialog appears, with a preview region at the right.

2. To arrange copies in a straight line, select **Create line**. For an X-by-Y grid arrangement, select **Create grid**.

3. Specify **Line length** (the number of objects including the original) in the arrangement, or the Grid size. Note that you can use the Line length setting to include an odd number of objects in a grid.

4. Set spacing between the objects as either an **Offset** (measured between the top left corners of successive objects) or a **Gap** (between the bottom right and top left corners). You can specify **Horizontal** and/or **Vertical** spacing, and/or an angular **Rotation**. To set a specific horizontal or vertical interval, check **Absolute**; uncheck the box to specify the interval as a percentage of the original object's dimensions.

5. Click **OK**.

The result is a multiple selection. Click its **Group** button if you want to keep the separate objects linked for additional manipulations.

Pasting an object's formatting

Once you have copied an object to the Clipboard, you can use **Paste Format** (**Edit** menu) to apply its formatting attributes to another **selected** object. Again from the **Edit** menu, **Paste Format Plus** displays a "master control" dialog that lets you select or deselect specific attributes to be included when formatting is pasted. See Saving object styles on p. 163 for more dialog information.

Moving objects

To move an object (including a multiple selection):

*   Drag the selected object by using its **Move** button. Once you see a move cursor you can begin dragging.

To set exact horizontal and vertical positions, use the Transform tab.

To constrain the movement of an object to horizontal or vertical:

- Select the object and use the keyboard arrows (up, down, left, right).

Resizing objects

WebPlus provides several methods of resizing lines, shapes, artistic text, frame objects, and table objects. Click-and-drag is the simplest—watch the Hintline for context-sensitive tips and shortcuts!

To resize an object (in general):

1. Select the object.

2. Click one of the object's handles and drag it to a new position while holding down the left mouse button.

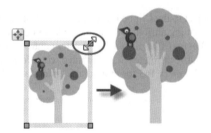

Dragging from an edge handle resizes in one dimension, by moving that edge. Dragging from a corner handle resizes in two dimensions, by moving two edges. You can also constrain the resizing—note that pictures normally behave differently from lines, shapes, and text objects.

★ Text in frames and tables doesn't change size when the container object is resized.

★ To set two or more objects to the same horizontal or vertical size as the last selected object, you can use **Arrange>Size Objects...**.

★ You can also make fine resizing adjustments from the Transform tab.

To resize freely:

- Drag from a corner (or line end) handle.

To constrain a shape, frame object, or table object when resizing:

- Hold the **Shift** key down and drag from a corner (or line end) handle.

For shapes, this has the effect of keeping a square as a square, a circle as a circle, etc.

> For pictures, dimensions are constrained on dragging a corner handle. Use **Shift**-drag to resize a picture freely.

Rotating an object

You can rotate single and multiple objects, including pictures, text objects, and groups using the Rotate Tool.

To rotate an object:

1. Select the ⟳ **Rotate Tool** on the **Tools** toolbar.

2. Click to select the object, hover over one of its handles until you see the rotate cursor (below).

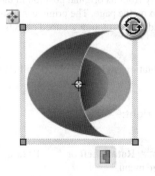

3. Hold the mouse button down and drag the cursor in the direction in which you want to rotate the object, then release (use the **Shift** key for 15° rotation intervals).

The Pointer Tool can also be used to rotate objects in the same way (with the ⤴ cursor).

To unrotate (restore the original orientation):

- Double-click the object.

- To restore the rotated position, double-click again.

To change the rotation origin:

1. Select the 🔄 **Rotate Tool** on the **Tools** toolbar and click to select the object.

2. Move the rotation origin ⊕ away from its original position in the center of the object to any position on the page. The origin can also be moved to be outside the object—ideal for rotating grouped objects around a central point.

3. Drag the rotate pointer to a new rotation angle—the object will rotate about the new pivot.

To rotate an object 90 degrees left or right:

- Select the object and choose the ◁ **Rotate Left** or ▷ **Rotate Right** command from the **Arrange** menu.

Cropping and combining objects

Cropping means masking (hiding) parts of an object, for example to improve composition or to create a special effect. The underlying object is intact. Two types of cropping are possible—**square** cropping or **irregular** cropping.

square crop   *irregular crop*

Combining starts with more than one object, but creates a special composite object with one or more "holes" on the inside where the component objects' fills overlapped one another—useful for creating mask or stencil effects.

To crop using the object's original outline:

1. Select the object, then select the ⬜ **Square Crop Tool** from the **Tools** toolbar's Effects flyout.

2. Drag one of its edge or corner handles inward for unconstrained cropping. Press the **Shift** key while dragging for constrained cropping (aspect ratio is maintained).

> To scale the object within the crop outline, **Ctrl**-drag either upwards or downwards.

To crop by modifying the object's outline:

• Select the object, then select the ⬜ **Irregular Crop Tool** from the **Tools** toolbar's Effects flyout. The Curve context toolbar appears, which lets you control the displayed nodes and connecting segments that define the object's crop outline. See Editing lines on p. 146.

- To move a node (control point) where you see the ⌐¦⌐ cursor, drag the node.

- ↖↶ To move a line segment (between two nodes) where you see the cursor, drag the segment.

To position a cropped object within its crop outline:

- With either crop tool selected, click the object and drag its center (when you see the hand cursor).

To feather the crop outline:

- With either crop tool selected, click the object.

- From the Crop context toolbar, set a **Feather** value using the up/down arrows, slider or by direct input. Feathering is applied outside the crop outline by the set point size.

To uncrop (restore full visibility):

- Click the **Remove Crop** button on the Crop context toolbar.

Cropping one shape to another

The **Crop to Shape** command works with exactly two objects selected. Either or both of these may be a group object. The lower object (the one behind the other) gets clipped to the outline of the upper object, leaving a shape equivalent to the overlapping region.

To crop one shape to another:

1. Place the "clipping" object in front of the object to be cropped, using the **Arrange** menu and/or **Arrange** toolbar as needed. In the illustration above, a QuickShape is in front of a text frame.

2. With both objects selected (or grouped), choose **Crop to Shape** from the **Tools** menu.

Combining lines and shapes

Combining curves is a way of creating a composite object from two or more lines or drawn shapes. As with cropping to a shape, the object in front clips the object(s) behind, in this case leaving one or more "holes" where the component objects overlapped. As with grouping, you can apply formatting (such as line or fill) to the combined object and continue to edit individual nodes and segments with the Pointer tool. Unlike those other methods, a combined object permanently takes the line and fill properties of the front object. Combining is reversible, but the component objects keep the line and fill properties of the combined object.

Combining is a quick way to create a mask or stencil cutout:

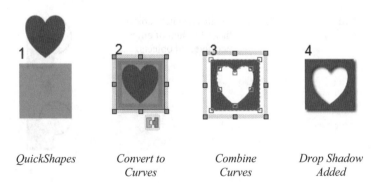

QuickShapes	*Convert to Curves*	*Combine Curves*	*Drop Shadow Added*

To combine two or more selected lines or drawn shapes:

1. Draw your two lines or QuickShapes.

2. Place the "clipping" object in front of the object to be cut out, using the **Arrange** menu and/or **Arrange** toolbar as needed.

3. Select each object and choose **Tools>Convert to Curves**.

4. Select both objects.

5. Choose **Combine Curves** from the **Arrange** menu.

To restore the original shapes from a combined object:

- Select the combined object and choose **Split Curves** from the **Arrange** menu.

Joining object outlines

WebPlus includes some powerful tools to carve new shapes out of old overlapping shapes. With add, subtract, intersect, or exclude commands you actually produce a permanent new object (with a new outline) out of any selected objects. The joined object can be further edited by adjusting nodes in the new shape.

To join outlines (selected via marquee selection):

- Select from the **Join Outlines** submenu on the **Arrange** menu.

Add	Creates one new object that's the sum of any two selected objects.	

Subtract

Discards the overlap
between the top and
bottom object. The
bottom object is also
discarded.

Useful as a quick way
of truncating shapes and
pictures with another
object.

Intersect

Retains the overlap and
discards the rest.

Exclude

Merges two or more
objects into a composite
object, with a clear
transparent "hole"
where their filled
regions overlap.

Locking an object's size or position

To prevent accidentally moving, resizing, flipping, or rotating an object, you can lock it in position.

To lock an object:

- Right-click on the object and choose **Arrange>Lock Objects**.

To unlock an object:

- Right-click on it and choose **Arrange>Unlock Objects**.

Ordering objects

As objects are created, they are **stacked** in the order you create them, from back to front, with each new object in front of the others. At any time, you can change the stacking order, which affects how objects appear on the page.

To shift the object's position one step toward the front or back:

- Click ▦ **Forward One** or ▦ **Back One** on the **Arrange** toolbar, respectively.

To shift the selected object's position to the bottom or top of the stack:

- Click ▦ **Send to Back** or ▦ **Bring to Front** on the **Arrange** toolbar, respectively.

Aligning and distributing objects

Alignment involves taking a group of selected objects and aligning them all in one operation by their top, bottom, left or right edges. You can also distribute objects, so that your objects (as a multiple selection) are spread evenly (optionally at spaced intervals).

Alignment or distribution can occur between the endmost objects on your page (current selection), page margins, or the page edge.

Alignment controls are available in either the Align tab or from **Arrange>Align Objects...**.

As other alignment options, tools such as **rulers** and the **snapping grid** provide guides to assist you in placing objects on the page. Snapping lets you align objects against sticky or non-sticky guides. For details, see Using layout aids and Snapping (p. 50 and p. 132).

To align the edges of two or more objects in a selection:

1. Using the Pointer Tool, **Shift**-click on all the objects you want to align, or draw a marquee box around them, to create a multiple selection.

2. Select the Align tab.

3. Select an option for vertical and/or horizontal alignment. Choose **Top**, **Bottom**, **Left**, **Right**, **Center Horizontally** or **Center Vertically**.

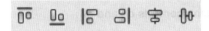

To distribute two or more objects:

- Choose **Space Evenly Across** or **Space Evenly Down** to spread selected objects uniformly between endmost objects in the current selection (horizontally or vertically, respectively) or by a set measurement (choose **Spaced** and set a value in any measurement unit).

Rather than work within the current selection area you can align or distribute to page margins (if set) or page edge.

To align/distribute objects to page margins or edges:

- Select from the **Relative to** drop-down menu to align the selected object(s) within the page **Margins** or **Page** edges then choose an align or distribute button described above.

Snapping

The **Snapping** feature simplifies placement and alignment by "magnetizing" moved or resized objects to grid dots and guide lines. Objects can also snap to other guides on the page such as page margins, rows, and columns (see p. 50), as well as the page edge, and page/margin centers (i.e., the center of the page in relation to the page edge or page margins). In addition, **dynamic guides** can be used to align and resize objects to existing object edges and centers by snapping. Guides appear dynamically as you drag objects.

To turn snapping on and off globally:

- Click ⊡ ▾ **Snapping** on the Hintline (don't click the drop-down arrow). The button has an orange color when snapping is switched on.

Once snapping is enabled, you can selectively switch on/off snapping options (i.e., Ruler Guides, Dot Grid, etc).

To turn individual snapping controls on and off:

- Click the down arrow on the ⊡ ▾ **Snapping** button (Hintline) and check/uncheck a snapping option via the drop-down menu.

★ The **Snapping** menu option offers the full set of snapping options for the user. You can also control **Snapping Distance**, i.e. the distance at which an object will start to snap to a dot, guide, etc.

★ For precise ruler guide placement, check **Snapping>Ruler Marks** in **Tools>Options** to snap guides to ruler marks.

Snapping with dynamic guides

For accurate object alignment and resizing, you can use **dynamic guides** instead of setting ruler guides manually or performing selection, transform, and alignment operations. These red-colored guides are shown between the vertices of the **last three selected** placed page objects and the manipulated object and "visually suggest" possible snapping options such as snap to the placed object's left, right, center, top, right, bottom, or to the page center. You can include objects to snap to by dragging over objects.

For alignment

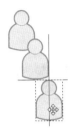

For resizing

To switch on dynamic guides:

- Click the down arrow on the **Snapping** button (Hintline) and click **Dynamic Guides** on the drop-down menu.

To snap to page centers as well, you must additionally check **Page center** in **Tools>Options>Layout>Snapping**.

Attaching objects to text

WebPlus lets you position shapes, pictures, or gallery objects in relation to your site's text (artistic or frame text) in one of two ways:

- **Float with text**. This option is ideal for pictures and shapes, etc.

*A shape attached
to artistic text such as titles*

*A picture within
a text frame*

- **Position inline as character**. The attached object is placed as a character in the text and vertically aligned in relation to the text that surrounds it.

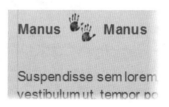

A gallery object attached to an artistic text title	*A "Fun" gallery object positioned inline within a text frame*

The advantage of both methods, is that the object associated with the text will move as your text is moved. For frame text especially, when the text reflows as new content is added to the frame, the attached object will move with the text.

To attach an object to text:

1. Position the object over or close to the artistic text or text frame to be attached to.

2. Select **Attach to Text...** from the **Arrange** menu.

3. From the dialog, choose a positioning option:

Either, for a **floating** object:

1. Enable **Float with text**. This is the default positioning option.

2. Set the **Position on text** option to set where the object is placed in relation to the artistic text or frame text. Select **Left** or **Right**, or set an **Indent by** value to left-indent by a set pixel value.

3. Once positioned, you can specify the **Distance from text**: the "standoff" between the object's outline and adjacent text.

4. Click **OK**.

Once attached, the object shows an ![] **Attach to Text** button under the object. Click to edit properties.

The ![] **Attach Point** is a set location in the artistic text or frame text from which the object is positioned from. Drag to a different position in the text to move the attach point and object simultaneously.

Or, for an **inline** object:

1. Enable **Position inline as character**.

2. To set the object's vertical alignment with respect to adjacent text, select an **Align with text** option. Text will not flow around the attached object.

3. (Optional) Enter a **Offset by** value to set the percentage to which the object will be vertically offset in relation to its height.

4. (Optional) Check **Scale to** to scale the object to a percentage of the adjacent text point size. This keeps the same relative size if the text size changes. 100% will scale precisely to current point size.

5. Once positioned, you can specify the **Distance from text**: the "standoff" between the object's outline and adjacent text.

4. (Optional) Check **Use these settings when pasting** to update floating and inline defaults. Any subsequent object pasting will adopt the settings saved when the option was checked.

5. Click **OK**. The object appears inline with text, and shows an ![] **Attach to Text** icon.

Objects inserted into text frames will automatically be attached using "Float with text" default settings.

To view attached object properties:

1. Select an attached object.

2. Click 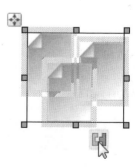 **Attach to Text** shown under the object.

The **Attached Object Properties** dialog is displayed. The options differ depending on which of the positioning options is enabled.

If you'd like to change the position of an attach point you can drag it anywhere else in your text frame. Dragging to an area away from the artistic text/text frame will disconnect your attached object. You can also disconnect the attach point via the Attached Object Properties dialog.

To disconnect an attached object:

*   From the Attached Object Properties dialog, enable **Detach from text**.

Notes

*   Attached objects have all the same properties of unattached objects; you can modify them whilst attached.

Creating groups

You can easily turn a multiple selection into a group object. When objects are grouped, you can position, resize, or rotate the objects all at the same time.

To create a group from a multiple selection:

*   Click the button.

To ungroup (turn a group back into a multiple selection):

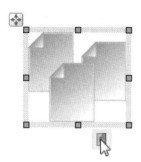

- Click the ![button] button. The group turns back to a multiple selection.

Simply clicking on any member of a group selects the group object. In general, any operation you carry out on a selected group affects each member of the group. However, the objects that comprise a group are intact, and you can also select and edit an individual object within a group.

To select an individual object within a group:

- **Ctrl**-click the object.

Updating and saving defaults

Object defaults are the stored property settings WebPlus applies to newly created objects such as:

- **lines** and **shapes** (line and fill color, shade, pattern, transparency, etc.)

- **frames** (margins, columns, etc.)

- **text** (i.e., font, size, color, alignment, etc.). Defaults are saved separately for **artistic, shape**, **frame** and **table text.**

You can easily change the defaults for any type of object via the **Update Object Default** command or the **Text Style Palette** dialog.

Default settings are always **local**—that is, any changed defaults apply to the current site and are automatically saved with it, so they're in effect next time you open that site. However, at any time you can use the **Save Defaults** command to record the current defaults as **global** settings that will be in effect for any new site you subsequently create.

To set local defaults for a particular type of object:

1. Create a single sample object and fine-tune its properties as desired—
or use an existing object that already has the right properties. (For
graphics, you can use a line, shape, or rectangle; all share the same set
of defaults.)

2. Select the object that's the basis for the new defaults and choose
Update Object Default from the **Format** menu.

Or, for line and fill colors, including line styles:

1. With no object selected, choose the required line and/or fill colors
from the Color or Swatches tab (see Applying solid colors on p. 209).
Use the Line tab to set a default line weight, style, and corner shape.

2. Draw your object on the page, which will automatically adopt the
newly defined default colors and styles.

To view and change default text properties:

1. Choose **Text Style Palette...** from the **Text** menu.

2. Click **Default Text**, then from the expanded list of text types, choose
an option (e.g., Artistic Text).

3. Click **Modify...** to view current settings for the selected text type.

4. Use the Text Style dialog to alter character, paragraph, and bullet/list
properties.

To save all current defaults as global settings:

1. Select **Save Defaults...** from the **Tools** menu.

2. From the dialog, check options to update specific defaults globally:

   - **Document and object defaults** - saves current site settings (page size, orientation) and object settings (context toolbar settings).

   - **Text styles** - saves current text styles in the Text Style Palette.

   - **Object styles** - saves user-defined styles from Styles tab.

   - **Table and calendar formats** - saves custom formats saved in Table Formats dialog.

3. Click **Save** to confirm that you want new publications to use the checked object's defaults globally.

8 Lines, Shapes, and Effects

Drawing and editing lines

WebPlus provides Pencil, Straight Line, and Pen tools for drawing freehand, straight, and curved/straight lines, respectively.

The  **Pencil Tool** lets you sketch curved lines and shapes in a **freeform** way.

The **Straight Line Tool** is for drawing **straight** lines; rules at the top and/or bottom of the page; or horizontal lines to separate sections or highlight headlines.

The 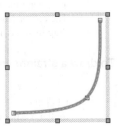 **Pen Tool** lets you join a series of line segments (which may be **curved** or **straight**) using "connect the dots" mouse clicks.

When selected, each line type shows square nodes which can be used for reshaping lines.

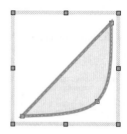

Any curved line can be closed (by joining line ends) to create a custom **shape** (see Drawing and editing shapes on p. 148 for details)

Drawing lines

To draw a freeform line (with the Pencil Tool):

1. Click the **Pencil Tool** from the **Standard Objects** toolbar's Line flyout.

2. Click where you want the line to start, and hold the mouse button down as you draw. The line appears immediately and follows your mouse movements.

3. To end the line, release the mouse button. The line will automatically smooth out using a minimal number of nodes.

4. To extend the line, position the cursor over one of its red end nodes. The cursor changes to include a plus symbol. Click on the node and drag to add a new line segment.

To draw a straight line (with the Straight Line Tool):

1. Click the **Straight Line Tool** from the **Standard Objects** toolbar's Line flyout.

2. Click where you want the line to start, and drag to the end point. The line appears immediately.

To constrain the angle of the straight line to 15° increments, hold down the **Shift** key as you drag. (This is an easy way to make exactly vertical or horizontal lines.)

3. To extend the line, position the cursor over one of its red end nodes. The cursor changes to include a plus symbol. Click on the node and drag to add a new line segment.

To draw one or more line segments (with the Pen Tool):

1. Click the 🖋 **Pen Tool** from the **Standard Objects** toolbar's Line flyout. On the Curve context toolbar, three buttons let you select which kind of segment to draw:

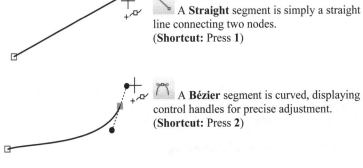

A **Straight** segment is simply a straight line connecting two nodes. (**Shortcut:** Press **1**)

A **Bézier** segment is curved, displaying control handles for precise adjustment. (**Shortcut:** Press **2**)

Smart segments appear without visible control handles, using automatic curve-fitting to connect each node. They are especially useful when tracing around curved objects and pictures. (**Shortcut:** Press **3**)

2. Select a segment type, then click where you want the line to start.

    - For a **Straight** segment, click again (or drag) for a new node where you want the segment to end. **Shift**-click to align the segment at 15° intervals (useful for quick right-angle junctions).

    - For a **Bézier** segment, click again for a new node and drag out a **control handle** from it. Click again where you want the segment to end, and a curved segment appears. The finished segment becomes selectable.

- For a **Smart** segment, click again for a new node. The segment appears as a smooth, best-fitting curve (without visible control handles) between the new node and the preceding node. Before releasing the mouse button, you can drag to "flex" the line as if bending a piece of wire. If the preceding corner node on the line is also smart, flexibility extends back to the preceding segment. You can **Shift**-click to create a new node that lines up at 15° intervals with the previous node.

3. To extend an existing line, repeat Step 2 for each new segment. Each segment can be of a different type.

4. To end the line, press **Esc**, double-click, or choose a different tool.

Editing lines

Use the Pointer Tool in conjunction with the Curve context toolbar to adjust lines once you've drawn them. The techniques are the same whether you're editing a separate line object or the outline of a closed shape.

See WebPlus help for information on editing lines.

Setting line properties

All lines, including those that enclose shapes, have numerous properties, including color, weight (width or thickness), scaling, cap (end), join (corner), and stroke alignment. You can vary these properties for any freehand, straight, or curved line, as well as for the outline of a shape (see Drawing and editing shapes on p. 148). Text frames, tables, and artistic text objects have line properties, too.

In WebPlus, you can control the position of the stroke (i.e., line width) in relation to the object's path, i.e. the line that defines the boundary of the object.

To change line properties of a selected object:

- Use the Swatches tab to change the line's color and/or shade. Alternatively, use the Color tab to apply a color to the selected object from a color mixer.

- Use the Line tab, context toolbar (shown when a line is selected), or Line and Border dialog to change the line's weight (thickness), type, or other properties. Select a line width, and use the drop-down boxes to pick the type of line. The context toolbar can also adjust line-end scaling as a percentage.

On the Line tab, context toolbar, or Line and Border dialog, the styles drop-down menu provides the following styles: **None**, **Single**, **Calligraphic**, and several **Dashed** and **Double** line styles as illustrated below.

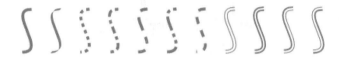

Several techniques offer additional ways to customize lines:

 For dotted/dashed lines, select from one of five line styles (see above).
OR
(tab and dialog only) Drag the **Dash Pattern** slider to set the overall pattern length (the number of boxes to the left of the slider) and the dash length (the number of those boxes that are black).

The illustrations below show lines with dash lengths of (**1**) 4 and 2, and (**2**) 5 and 4:

 For double lines, select from one of four **Double** line styles (see above).

(Tab only) For calligraphic lines of variable width (drawn as if with a square-tipped pen held at a certain angle), select the calligraphic line style (opposite) from the drop-down menu, then use the **Calligraphic Angle** box to set the angle of the pen tip, as depicted in the examples below.

You can also vary a line's **Cap** (end) and the **Join** (corner) where two lines intersect.

Drawing and editing shapes

QuickShapes are pre-designed objects of widely varying shapes that you can instantly add to your page.

Once you've drawn a QuickShape, you can morph its original shape using control handles, and adjust its properties—for example, by applying gradient or bitmap fills (including your own bitmap pictures!) or apply transparency effects.

Another way to create a shape is to draw a line (or series of line segments) and then connect its start and end nodes, creating a closed shape.

QuickShapes

The QuickShape flyout contains a wide variety of commonly used shapes, including boxes, ovals, arrows, polygons and stars.

You can easily turn shapes into web **buttons** by adding hyperlinks or overlaying hotspots. The "QuickButton" (indicated) is especially intended for creating stylish button outlines!

It's also possible to use the always-at-hand QuickShape context toolbar situated above the workspace to adjust a QuickShape's line weight, color, style, and more. New shapes always take the default line and fill (initially a black line with no fill).

To create a QuickShape:

1. Click the ▢ ▼ **QuickShape** flyout on the **Standard Objects** toolbar and select a shape. The button takes on the icon of the shape you selected.

2. Click on the page to create a new shape at a default size.
   OR
   Drag across the page to size your shape. When the shape is the right size, release the mouse button.

To draw a constrained shape (such as a circle):

* Hold down the **Shift** key as you drag.

All QuickShapes can be positioned, resized, rotated, and filled. What's more, you can morph them using adjustable sliding handles around the QuickShape. Each shape changes in a logical way to allow its exact appearance to be altered.

To adjust the appearance of a QuickShape:

1. Click on the QuickShape to reveal one or more sliding handles around the shape. These are distinct from the "inner" selection handles. Different QuickShapes have different handles which have separate functions.

2. To change the appearance of a QuickShape, drag its handles.

★ To find out what each handle does for a particular shape, move the Pointer Tool over the handle and read the Hintline.

Closed shapes

As soon as you draw or select a line, you'll see the line's nodes appear. Nodes show the end points of each segment in the line. Freehand curves typically have many nodes; straight or curved line segments have only two (**1**). You can make a shape by drawing a line between node end points (**2**), or by simply closing the curve (**3**).

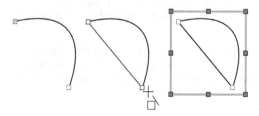

To turn a selected line into a shape:

- Select the line with the Pointer Tool and click the Close Curve button on the Curve context toolbar.

You can go the other way, too—break open a shape in order to add one or more line segments.

To break open a line or shape:

1. With the Pointer Tool, select the node where you want to break the shape.

2. Click the Break Curve button on the Curve context toolbar. A line will separate into two lines. A shape will become a line, with the selected node split into two nodes, one at each end of the new line.

3. You can now use the Pointer Tool to reshape the line as needed.

See online Help for information on editing shapes.

Using 2D filter effects

WebPlus provides a variety of **filter effects** that you can use to transform any object. "3D" filter effects let you create the impression of a textured surface and are covered elsewhere (see p. 154). Here we'll look at 2D filter effects exclusively. The following examples show each 2D filter effect when applied to the letter "A."

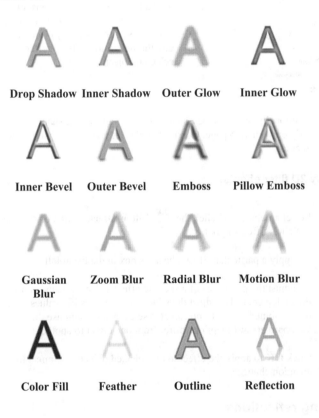

Drop Shadow Inner Shadow Outer Glow Inner Glow

Inner Bevel Outer Bevel Emboss Pillow Emboss

Gaussian Zoom Blur Radial Blur Motion Blur
Blur

Color Fill Feather Outline Reflection

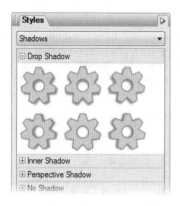

The Studio's **Styles tab** offers a range of 2D filter effects that are ready to use. Its multiple categories each offer a gallery full of predefined effects, such as shadows, bevels, reflections, blurs, and more. Each category offers subtle variations of the category effect. Click any thumbnail to apply the effect to the selected object.

WebPlus additionally provides the Shadow Tool for applying a shadow to an object directly on your web page. Control handles let you adjust shadow blur, opacity and color.

To apply 2D filter effects:

1. Select an object and click the *fx* **Filter Effects** button on the **Tools** toolbar's Effects flyout.

2. To apply a particular effect, check its box in the list at left.

3. To adjust the properties of a specific effect, select its name and vary the dialog controls. Adjust the sliders or enter specific values to vary the combined effect. (You can also select a slider and use the keyboard arrows.) Options differ from one effect to another.

4. Click **OK** to apply the effect to the selected object, or **Cancel** to abandon changes.

Creating reflections

A simple way to add creative flair to your page is to apply a vertical reflection on a selected object. The effect is especially eye-catching when applied to pictures, but can be equally impressive on artistic text, such as page titles or text banners. A combination of settings can control reflection height, opacity, offset and blurring.

Creating outlines

WebPlus lets you create a colored outline around objects, especially text and shapes (as a **filter effect**). For any outline, you can set the outline width, color fill, transparency, and blend mode. The outline can also take a gradient fill, a unique **contour** fill (fill runs from the inner to outer edge of the outline width), or pattern fill and can also sit inside, outside, or be centered on the object edge.

As with all effects you can switch the outline effect on and off. You'll be able to apply a combination of 2D or 3D filter effects along with your outline, by checking other options in the Filter Effects dialog.

Using the Shadow Tool

Shadows are great for adding flair and dimension to your work, particularly to pictures and text objects, but also to shapes, text frames and tables. To help you create them quickly and easily, WebPlus provides the **Shadow Tool** on the **Tools** toolbar's Effects flyout. The tool affords freeform control of the shadow effect allowing creation of adjustable **basic** or **skewed edge-based shadows** for any WebPlus object.

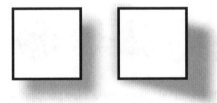

Basic (left) and skewed shadows (right) applied to a square QuickShape.

Adjustment of shadow color, opacity, blur, and scaling/distance is possible using controllable nodes directly on the page (or via a supporting Shadow context toolbar). Nodes can be dragged inwards or outwards from the shadow origin to modify the shadow's blur and opacity. For a different color, select the Color node then pick a new color from the Color or Swatches tab. Depending on if a basic or skewed shadow is required, the origin can exist in the center (shown) or at the edge of an object, respectively.

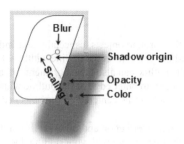

Once you've created a shadow, you can also fine-tune it as needed using the Filter Effects dialog.

Using 3D filter effects

3D filter effects go beyond 2D filter effects (such as shadow, glow, bevel, and emboss effects) to create the impression of a textured surface on the object itself. You can use the **Filter Effects** dialog to apply one or more effects to the same object. Keep in mind that none of these 3D effects will "do" anything to an unfilled object—you'll need to have a fill there to see the difference they make!

The Studio's Styles tab is a good place to begin experimenting with 3D filter effects. Its multiple categories each offers a gallery full of pre-defined mixed 2D and 3D effects, using various settings.

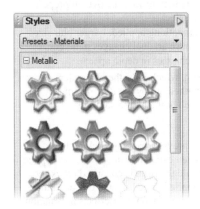

There you'll see a variety of remarkable 3D surface and texture presets in various categories (Glass, Metallic, Wood, etc.). Click any thumbnail to apply it to the selected object. Assuming the object has some color on it to start with, you'll see an instant result!

fx Alternatively, you can customize a Styles tab preset, or apply one or more specific effects from scratch, by using **Filter Effects**.

To apply 3D filter effects:

1. Click *fx* **Filter Effects** on the **Tools** toolbar's Effects flyout.

2. Check the **3D Effects** box at the left. The **3D Lighting** box is checked by default.

- **3D Effects** is a master switch, and its settings of **Blur** and **Depth** make a great difference; you can click the "+" button to unlink them for independent adjustment.

- **3D Lighting** provides a "light source" without which any depth information in the effect wouldn't be visible. The lighting settings let you illuminate your 3D landscape and vary its reflective properties.

✔ 3D Effects
 3D Bump Map
  Function
   Advanced
 2D Bump Map
 3D Pattern Map
  Function
   Advanced
 2D Pattern Map
 Transparency
✔ 3D Lighting

3. Adjust the "master control" sliders here to vary the overall properties of any individual 3D effects you select.

    • **Blur** specifies the amount of smoothing applied. Larger blur sizes give the impression of broader, more gradual changes in height.

    • **Depth** specifies how steep the changes in depth appear.

    • The ⊞ button is normally down, which links the two sliders so that sharp changes in Depth are smoothed out by the Blur parameter. To adjust the sliders independently, click the button so it's up.

4. (Optional) If needed, expand the preview pane by clicking the ▷ **Show/Hide Preview** button. When expanded, the effects are applied only in the preview window. While the pane is collapsed (click the button again), filter effects are applied directly to the object on the page. The former approach lets you work on your effects in isolation without other page objects interfering while fine-tuning your effects. Use zoom in/out buttons or a percentage magnification for detailed work.

5. Check a 3D effect in the 3D Effects list and experiment with the available settings.

Adding dimensionality (Instant 3D)

Using the **Instant 3D** feature, you can easily transform flat shapes (shown) and text into three-dimensional objects.

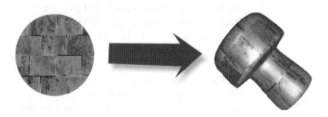

WebPlus provides control over 3D effect settings such as:

•   **bevelling**: use several rounded and chiselled presets or create your own with a custom bevel profile editor.

•   **lighting**: up to eight editable and separately colored lights can be positioned to produce dramatic lighting effects.

- **lathe effects**: create contoured objects (e.g., a bottle cork) with the custom lathe profile editor and extrusion control.

- **texture**: control how texture is extruded on objects with non-solid fills.

- **viewing**: rotate your object in three dimensions.

- **material**: controls the extent to which lighting has an effect on the object's surfaces (great for 3D artistic text!).

An always-at-hand 3D context toolbar hosted above your workspace lets you configure the above settings—each setting contributes to the 3D effect applied to the selected object. For on-the-page object control you can transform in 3D with use of a red orbit circle, which acts as an axis from which you can rotate around the X-, Y-, and Z-axes in relation to your page. Look for the cursor changing as you hover over the red circles' nodes or wire frame.

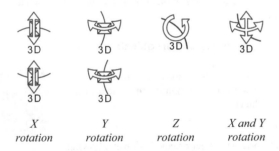

X	*Y*	*Z*	*X and Y*
rotation	*rotation*	*rotation*	*rotation*

Transform about your 3D objects' axes instead of your pages' axes by holding the **Ctrl** key down as you transform.

You can also adjust the angle and elevation of each "active" light on the page by dragging the light pointer to a position which simulates a light source.

After any transformation, the underlying base object remains editable.

To add dimensionality:

1. Select an object and click the 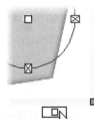 **Instant 3D** button from the **Tools** toolbar's Effects flyout. The object immediately adopts 3D characteristics with a red orbit circle displayed in the object's foreground.

2. Click a 3D effect category from the first drop-down menu on the 3D context toolbar; the bar's options change dynamically according to the category currently selected. See the online Help for more details.

> Click **Reset Defaults** on the context toolbar to revert to the object back to its initial transformation.

To switch off 3D effects:

*   Click the **Remove 3D** button on the context toolbar. You can always click the Tool toolbar's **Instant 3D** button at any time later to reinstate the effect.

To edit base properties of a 3D object:

*   Select the 3D object, then click the **Edit** button at the bottom right-hand corner of the 3D object.

    The original object's shape is shown, allowing its selection handles to be manipulated for resizing and rotating.

Adding borders

Lorem Ipsum
Curabitur felis erat, tempus eu,
placerat et, pellentesque sed,
purus. Sed sed diam. Nam nunc.
Class aptent taciti sociosqu ad
litora torquent per conubia
nostra, per inceptos hymenaeos.

A **border** is a repeating, decorative element that can be set to enclose objects, such as text frames, pictures, and tables.

WebPlus comes with an impressive range of categorized picture-based border styles for you to use. However, if you'd like to create your own **custom** borders you can import a border design as a picture, and save it for future use.

Edge selection lets you apply the border effect to all sides, top, bottom, left, right, or both top and bottom (opposite).

> The Picture Frames category in the Gallery tab offers the same set of border styles but already applied to placeholder picture frames. (See p. 67.)

To add a border to an object:

1. Click **Line/Border** on the **Tools** toolbar's Fill flyout.

2. To define the border, select the **Border** tab, then select a border preset from the **Style** drop-down list. You can preview each border in the window at the right as you scroll down the open list with your keyboard up/down arrows.

    To remove a border, select **None** from the top of the list.

3. Select a border **Weight** (width) for your border. You may need to experiment to find a width that complements the size of your object.

4. To apply the border to specific edges of the object, use the **Edge** drop-down menu.

You can switch edges on and off to make multiple combinations.

5. Set other options as needed:

    *   Select a border **Type**. **Tile** repeats the edge design, **Stretch** simply stretches the design; **Single** scales the original picture to fit the object. Each preset's Type is already set so you may only need to adjust this for your own custom borders.

    *   Select an **Alignment** setting to fit the border to the **Outside**, **Inside**, or **Middle** of the object's bounding box.

    *   If **Behind contents** is checked, the inner half of the border extends behind the object. If unchecked, the whole border appears in front (the wider the border, the more it encroaches on the filled region).

    *   If **Scale with object** is checked, both border and object change together when you resize the object. If unchecked, the border weight remains constant during resizing.

    *   If **Draw center** is unchecked (the default), the inside areas of a framed picture (used to create your new border) will be left empty, so you won't need to manually remove unwanted image centers. When checked, the area inside a populated custom frame is repeated.

6. Click **OK** when you're done.

Use the **Import** button to base your borders on your own bordered picture design.

Once you've optimized the design of your new border, you might like to save it for future use. The border is stored globally so you can make use of it in other publications.

To save your custom border:

1. Click **Save as...**

2. From the dialog, select a subcategory (e.g., Fun, Fabric, etc.) from the drop-down list; alternatively, enter a new custom subcategory name in the box.

3. From the dialog, enter your custom border name. The new border appears in the Line and Border dialog's **Style** drop-down list (and also as a categorized bordered picture frame in the Gallery tab).

Using object styles

Object styles benefit your design efforts in much the same way as text styles and color schemes. Once you've come up with a set of attributes that you like—properties like line color, fill, border, and so on—you can save this cluster of attributes as a named style. WebPlus remembers which objects are using that style, and the style appears in the **Styles tab**, and can subsequently be applied to new objects.

Here's how object styles work to your advantage:

●   Each object style can include settings for a host of object attributes, such as line color, line style, fill, transparency, filter effects, font, and border. The freedom to include or exclude certain attributes, and the nearly unlimited range of choices for each attribute, makes this a powerful tool in the designer's arsenal.

- Any time you want to alter some aspect of the style (for example, change the line color), you simply change the style definition. Instantly, all objects in your site sharing that style update accordingly.

- Object styles you've saved globally appear not only in the original site but in any new site, so you can reuse exactly the same attractive combination of attributes for any subsequent design effort.

The Styles tab contains multiple galleries of pre-designed styles that you can apply to any object, or customize to suit your own taste! Galleries exist in effect categories such as Blurs, 3D, Edge, Warps, Shadows, Materials (e.g., metals) and more, with each category having further subcategories.

To apply an object style to one or more objects:

1. Display the **Styles** tab.

2. Expand the drop-down menu to select a named style category (e.g., Blurs), then pick a subcategory by scrolling the lower window.

3. Preview available styles as thumbnails (cog shapes are shown by default) in the window.

4. Click a style thumbnail to apply it to the selected object(s).

To remove an object style from a gallery:

- Right-click the thumbnail and choose **Delete**.

To unlink an object from its style definition:

- Right-click the object and choose **Format>Object Style>Unlink**.

If you've applied a style to an object but have lost track of the thumbnail—or want to confirm which style is actually being used on an object—you can quickly locate the thumbnail from the object.

To locate an object's style in the Styles tab:

- Right-click the object and choose **Format>Object Style>Locate in Studio**.

The Styles tab displays the gallery thumbnail for the object's style.

Normally, a site's object styles are just stored locally—that is, as part of that site; they don't automatically carry over to new sites. If you've created a new style you'll want to use in another site, you can save it globally so that it will appear in the Styles tab each time you open a new site.

Saving Object Styles

To create a new object style based on an existing object's attributes:

1. Right-click the object and choose **Format>Object Style>Create**.

2. The Style Attributes Editor dialog appears, with a tree listing object attributes on the left and a preview region on the right (not shown).

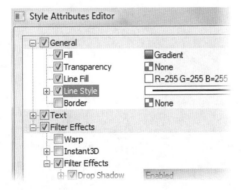

3. Click to expand or collapse sections within the attributes tree. Check any attributes you want to include in the style definition, and uncheck any you don't want to include.

4. If you want to change any of the current object settings, double-click an attribute (or select it and click the **Edit** button). This will bring up a detailed dialog for the particular attribute.

5.   The **Object** pane in the preview region shows the currently selected object after applying the defined style. Select the **Artistic Text** or **Frame Text** tab to see the style applied to sample objects of those types.

6.   Click the **Browse...** button to select the gallery category where you want to locate the style thumbnail, and optionally, save to a different Preview Type (Rounded Rectangle, Frame Text, or Artistic Text) instead of the default cog shape.

7.   Type a name to identify the gallery thumbnail.

8.   Click **OK**. A thumbnail for the new object style appears in the gallery.

Once an object style is listed in a gallery, you can modify it or create a copy by right-clicking on its thumbnail and choosing **Edit...** or **Copy...**.

To save a site's object styles globally:

1.   Choose **Save Defaults...** from the **Tools** menu.

2.   From the dialog, check **Object styles**, then click **Save**.

9 Images, Animation, and Multimedia

Adding picture frames

Not to be confused with a decorative border, a **picture frame** is a shaped container similar to a text frame. You can select either:

- **Bordered** picture frames from the Gallery tab.

  OR

- **Borderless** frames from the **Tools** toolbar.

WebPlus lets you import a picture directly into the frame or drag a picture into it from the Media bar. Empty picture frames are shown as envelope-shaped placeholders. At any time you can replace the picture in the frame.

All selected picture frames that contain a picture will display a supporting Picture frame toolbar under the frame. This offers panning, rotation (90 degrees counter-clockwise), zoom in, zoom out, and replace picture controls).

To add a bordered picture frame:

1. From the Gallery tab, select **Picture Frames** in the drop-down list.

2. Scroll to a sub-category (e.g., Metallic, Natural) of your choice.

3. Drag the frame design thumbnail to your page.

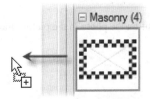

To add a borderless picture frame:

1. For an empty square frame, choose **Picture>Empty Frame...** from the **Insert** menu.

2. ▦ The mouse pointer changes to the **Picture Paste** cursor. What you do next determines the initial size and placement of the picture frame.

3. To insert the frame at a default size, simply click the mouse.
   OR
   To set the size of the frame, drag out a region and release the mouse button.

To add a picture to a frame:

- From the Media bar's currently displayed album, drag and drop a photo directly onto the picture frame.
  OR

  Click 🖾 **Replace Picture** directly under the selected frame, locate and select an image. Click **Open**.

★ Take advantage of the Gallery tab to drag and drop various bordered and basic picture frames onto your page. Choose from frames of different orientations and styles.

The picture is added to the frame using default Picture Frame properties, i.e. it is scaled to maximum fit; aspect ratio is always maintained. However, you can alter the picture's size, orientation and positioning relative to its frame.

To change picture size and positioning:

Select a populated picture frame, and from the accompanying Picture Frame toolbar:

- Click the 🖾 button to position the photo in the picture frame by panning.

- Click the button to rotate the photo in 90 degree counter-clockwise increments.

- Click the button to zoom in/out of the photo.

OR

1. Right-click on a picture frame and choose **Properties>Frame Properties...**.
    OR
    Select the picture frame and choose **Frame Properties** on the Picture context toolbar.

2. In the dialog, you can scale to maximum/minimum, **Stretch to Fit**, or use the original image's size (**No Scale**).

3. To change vertical alignment of pictures within the frames, select **Top**, **Middle**, or **Bottom**.

4. For horizontal alignment, select **Left**, **Center**, or **Right**.

Importing images

WebPlus lets you insert images from a wide variety of file formats. Here's a quick overview:

- **Bitmapped** images, also known as **bitmaps** or **raster** images, are built from a matrix of dots ("pixels"), rather like the squares on a sheet of graph paper. They may originate as digital camera photos or scanned images, or be created (or enhanced) with a "paint" program or photo editor. Typical examples include gif, jpg, png, and wdp.

- **Draw** graphics, also known as **vector** images, are resolution-independent and contain drawing commands such as "draw a line from A to B."

- **Metafiles** are the native graphics format for Windows and combine raster and vector information. Serif also has its own metafile format, Serif MetaFile Format (SMF), which is optimized for image sharing between Serif applications.

You can also acquire images directly from PhotoCDs or via TWAIN devices (scanners or digital cameras).

Inserting images

There are several ways to bring an image into WebPlus. You can drag a file from an external Windows folder directly onto your page, drag a thumbnail from WebPlus's Media Bar (see p. 174), paste from the pasteboard, or import an image as a file via a dialog.

- **Detached** images float freely on a page, while **inline** images are incorporated with the text flow in a text object.

- **Embedded** images become part of the WebPlus site, while **linking** places a reference copy of the image on the page and preserves a connection to the original file. Each approach has its pros and cons (see Embedding vs. Linking on p. 173).

WebPlus lets you place your image onto the page at its original size. The image will be uncropped by default but you have the option to crop the image, and adjust the image's picture frame properties with respect to image positioning and scaling within the picture frame.

To add an image from the Media Bar:

- Drag an image thumbnail onto the page from the currently displayed album(s) shown in WebPlus's Media Bar (expand the Media Bar from the bottom of your workspace). You can also drag onto an existing image to replace it.

To import an image from a file:

1. (Optional) If you want to place the image inline, click for an insertion point in a text object. For a detached image, make sure text objects are deselected.

2. **In the main window**:

    • Click the   **Import Picture...** button on the **Standard Objects** toolbar's Picture flyout.

    In WritePlus:
    • Choose **Picture File...** from the **Insert** menu.

3. Use the **Import Picture** dialog to select the image file to open.

4. Select either **Embed Picture** or **Link Picture**. See Embedding vs. linking on p. 173.

5. Click **Open**.

If you've opened an image via the QuickBuilder Bar, the image will automatically display on the page.

---

6. If there's a text insertion point in the main window, you'll be prompted whether to insert the image at the current cursor position. Click **Yes** if that's what you want.

    If there was no insertion point (or you answer "No" to the insertion prompt), you'll see the mouse pointer change to the **Picture Paste** cursor. What you do next determines the initial size and placement of the detached image.

7. To insert the image at its original pixel size, simply click the mouse.
    OR
    To set the size of the inserted image, drag out a region and release the mouse button. Use the **Shift** key for unconstrained placement (normal operation is to maintain the image's aspect ratio).

For multi-image pasting, select multiple images in the Open dialog, then paste each image one by one onto the page (by consecutive clicks).

Replacing images

The replace picture option lets you swap an image at any time, especially useful when you want to retain an image's position and dimensions on the page but want to update the image itself. It can be used on any image (uncropped or cropped).

To replace an image:

*   Click the ⬚ **Replace Picture** button directly under the selected image, locate and select an image. Click **Open**.

To replace an image via Media Bar:

- Drag an image thumbnail onto an existing image from the currently displayed album(s) shown in WebPlus's Media Bar (expand the Media Bar from the bottom of your workspace first).

Adjusting cropped images

WebPlus provides additional options for working with cropped images—either pictures you've cropped with the Crop tools (Tools toolbar) or replaceable pictures already present in design templates. For example, you can pan or zoom to adjust the portion of the image that displays inside its "frame," or you can change the way the image is scaled and aligned by adjusting its frame properties.

When you select a cropped image with the **Pointer Tool**, a control bar displays below the image, offering panning, rotation, zoom in, zoom out, and replace picture options.

- To reposition a cropped image inside its "frame," click 🖐, and then click and drag on the image.

- To rotate an image in 90° counter-clockwise increments, click the 🔄 button.

- To zoom in or out of an image, click one of the ⊕ ⊖ zoom in/out tools.

- To replace an image, click 🖼, then browse to locate the new image and click **Open**.

To alter frame properties:

1. Right-click on a cropped image and choose **Frame Properties....**
   OR
   Select the image and choose **Frame Properties** on the Picture context toolbar.

2. In the dialog, you can scale to maximum/minimum, **Stretch to Fit**, or use the original image's size (**No Scale**).

3. To change the vertical alignment of the image within the frame, select **Top**, **Middle**, or **Bottom**.

4. For horizontal alignment, select **Left**, **Center**, or **Right**.

Selecting an uncropped picture offers only a Replace Picture button.

Embedding vs. linking

Embedding means the image in WebPlus is now distinct from the original file. Embedding results in a larger WebPlus file, and if you need to alter an embedded image you'll need to re-import it after editing. Still, it's the best choice if file size isn't an issue and graphics are final.

Linking inserts a copy of the image file into the WebPlus site, linked to the actual file so that any changes you later make to it in the native application will be automatically reflected in WebPlus. Linking is one way of avoiding "bloat" by limiting the size of the site file. On the other hand, you'll need to manage the externally linked files carefully, for example making sure to include them all if you move the WebPlus file to a different drive.

Either option does not affect your published website, only your WebPlus site.

By default, WebPlus prompts you to embed images that are <256 KB, by pre-selecting the "Embed Picture" option in the **Insert** Picture dialog (but you can always select "Link Picture" instead). If you like, you can change the threshold file size or even switch off the automatic selection.

You can check resources via Site Manager later on, to change an item's status from linked to embedded, or vice versa.

For dragging images from the Media Bar, images <256 KB are embedded, while images >256 KB are linked. However, you can change embed or link status with the **Shift** key as you drag.

To preselect embedding or linking based on file size:

1. Choose **Options...** from the **Tools** menu. Select the **General** menu option.

2. To preselect the "Embed Picture" option for images under a certain size, select the threshold size in the "Embed if smaller than" list. ("Link Picture" will be pre-selected for images larger than the threshold.)

3. To choose whether to embed or link each image, uncheck **Suggest embed/link picture**. You can still select either option in the import dialog; it will now remember and preselect the last setting you used.

Using the Media Bar

The Media Bar acts as a "basket" containing photos for inclusion in your site. Its chief use is to aid the design process by improving efficiency (avoiding having to import photos one by one) and convenience (making photos always-at-hand). For photo-rich websites in particular, perhaps based on a WebPlus design templates, the Media Bar is a valuable tool for dragging photos directly onto unwanted pictures to replace them.

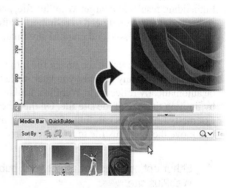

The Media Bar can be used as a temporary storage area before placing photos in your site, or it can be used to create more permanent photo albums from which you can retrieve stored photos at any time. By default, photos are added to a **temporary album** but remember to click the **New Album** button if you want to save your album for later use. Each time you start WebPlus you simply load that saved album (or any other saved album) or just work with a temporary album—the choice is yours!

You can import an unlimited number of photos by file or by whole folders, and whether photos are embedded or linked to your site in advance of photo placement on the page.

For large photo collections, searching throughout albums for photos by file name and EXIF, IPTC or XMP metadata is possible; even edit XMP metadata from within WebPlus.

> ★ The currently loaded album shown on your Media Bar will remain visible irrespective of which site you have open.

Thumbnails can be dragged from the Media Bar directly onto an existing picture on your page, replacing it in the process. Alternatively, a picture can be added as new, being placed at its original size.

To view the Media Bar:

- Unless already displayed, click the ▬▬▲▬▬ handle at the bottom of your workspace.

To add photos to a temporary album:

1. With the Media Bar visible and a temporary album loaded, click on the Media Bar's workspace to reveal an **Import Picture** dialog.

2. From the dialog, navigate to a folder, then select photo(s) for import. Photos are linked by default.

3. Click **Open**. Your photos appear as thumbnails in the Media Bar workspace.

> ★ Unless you save it, the temporary album and its photo contents will not be saved when you close WebPlus.

> 📖 You can drag one or more files from any Windows folder directly into the Media Bar window. If you right-click an image in the Media Bar and choose **Locate in Explorer** you'll open the photo's folder via Windows Explorer—great for drag and drop or just general file management!

To save a temporary album to a named album:

1. Click the down arrow on the **Add To** button. From the menu, select **New Album**.

2. In the **New Album** dialog, in the **Album Name** box, type a name to identify your album in the future.

3. (Optional) For any photo you can alter the resolution (native or 96 dpi), or embed/link status in advance of placement on your page—click a photo's setting (DPI, Placement) and use the setting's drop-down menu to change. You can also change these settings during drag/drop onto the page.

4. Click **OK**.

To include a temporary album's photos in an existing saved album, click the **Add To** button and choose a named album from the menu.

To create a named album:

1. Click the bar's **New Album** button.

2. In the dialog, in the **Album Name** box, type a name to identify your album in the future.

3. Click the **Add Image...** or **Add Folder...** button.

4. In the dialog, navigate to a photo or folder and optionally choose whether your photos are to be placed at native or 96 dpi, or embedded or linked (embedding increases your file size significantly). Click **Open**.

5. The **New Album** dialog lists the files for inclusion. Optionally, alter DPI and Embed options by clicking on each photo's setting, then selecting from the drop-down menu.

6. Click **OK**.

To load a saved album:

- Select a saved album name from the bar's top-right drop-down menu. The album's photos will display in the workspace.

A saved album can be selected as above and then modified via the **Manage** button (only shown for existing saved albums). You can add photos/folders, delete photos, change DPI, and alter embed/link status.

To rename or delete an album:

- Right-click an existing album name in the top-right drop-down menu and choose **Rename Album** or **Delete Album**.

To sort results from an album:

- In the **Sort By** search box, choose Filename, Rating, or Date Taken to reorder the photos accordingly to option.

Adding photos to the page

To add a photo to your page:

1. Display the Media Bar's temporary album or load a saved album from the top-right drop-down menu.

2. Drag an album's photo thumbnail onto the page and release your mouse button.

Setting image export options

When you publish your site, WebPlus applies certain global settings to determine how each image—whether drawn, pasted in, or imported—ends up as a separate bitmap displayed on the web page.

Here's a quick summary of the conversion settings as they're initially defined for web publishing:

- Each referenced image is exported as a separate file.

- Any image you inserted as a GIF, JPEG, or PNG is exported as the original file, using its original file name.

- Inserted metafiles and all other graphics are regenerated as PNG images.

You can alter these settings, but before doing so you should review the "logic" WebPlus applies to publishing web graphics. First, WebPlus has one **default format** to which **all** graphics will be converted on export—but you can make exceptions to this rule by specifying that certain image types should remain as their original file. Initially, PNG is the default format, but with **overrides** set for GIFs and JPEGs. That's why, using the initial settings above, GIFs stay as they are while all other graphics get converted to PNGs.

You can check and change these settings in the **Site Properties** dialog (**File** menu). The settings there are global and apply to all graphics in the site—but again you can make exceptions, in this case for individual graphics. To do so, for a selected graphic you could:

- Use the **Image Export Options...** (**Format** menu) or the **Image Export Manager** (**Tools** menu) to set the export format of particular images on a case-by-case basis.
  OR
  Convert certain images to a specific format beforehand using the **Tools>Convert to Picture**.

This combination of global and local settings gives you almost total control (if you care to exercise it) over how your graphics make it onto your web pages! Let's look first at how the global settings work.

To set global export options for web graphics:

1. Choose **Site Properties...** from the **File** menu and select the **Graphics** tab.

2. In the **Export File Format** section, select a preferred export format. This is the default format to which all graphics will be converted on export unless you set overrides. For JPGs, you can set a compression value. For PNGs, **Use PNG transparency** and **Use compatibility hack..** options allow PNG transparency and properly render PNG alpha transparency (in Internet Explorer 5.5 and 6.0), respectively.

3. In the **Resampling** section, choose a resampling method to give Best Quality, Sharper, or Smoother images of any format; the better quality, the slower the export. Check the **Don't resample pictures...** option to avoid resampling on images when exported image size will be approximate to original image size.

4. For exporting original graphic file names, in the **Naming** section check **Use original names of picture files**. Graphics will be stored in the root of your published website.

5. In the **Optimization** section, keep **Combine overlapping graphics into a single file** checked to have WebPlus analyze the site and (where a smaller file would result) output overlapping graphics as a single graphic. Whether this option makes sense will depend on your particular layout. Rather than use this global approach, you might consider using **Tools>Convert to Picture** in specific cases.

Setting export options, title, and alternate text for individual graphics

The **Image Export Manager** is a Wizard that lets you set the export file format for individual graphics in the site, or for objects such as rotated text that will be converted to images on export. These local, image-by-image settings **override** the global settings (as set in **File>Site Properties**) which WebPlus uses to determine the export format. You can run the Wizard to check a single selected image, the current page, or the entire site. For each image, you can save it using different methods. Either:

*   Choose a specific format (GIF, JPEG, or PNG) to export to (or just defer to site default settings). For JPEG, you can choose a level of compression.
    OR

*   Save the file to a chosen path and file name on export. Perhaps you want to add more meaningful descriptive names to images on export (especially useful when maintaining your website) instead of having the images export with automatically generated image names.

Let your own eye be the judge. Your best bet is to retain the **Use site default settings** option for all images to start with. Using the original global settings, this means that GIFs, JPEGs, and PNGs will be exported as their original files, while any others, including QuickShapes and closed shapes, will be published as PNGs. Then preview your site and determine if you want to vary the global settings or try a different output format for specific images.

Even if you don't change any format settings, you can set a picture **title** which will normally appear as a tooltip when the image is moused over in a browser. You can also enter **alternate text** (manually or automatically) for accessibility reasons.

To set export format, title, and/or alternate text:

1. If you're checking just a single image, you can select it first and choose **Image Export Options...** from the **Format** or right-click menu.
    OR
    To review web export options for images throughout your site, choose **Image Export Manager...** from the **Tools** menu.

2. (Only if you're using the Image Export Manager) Select whether you are checking a selected object, current page or entire site in the Wizard, then click **Continue**. The Wizard cycles through graphics in the specified range, and displays each one in turn along with the Image Export Options dialog.

3. In the dialog's **Save Picture As** section, you can choose to enable either:

    *   **Save to a format and name chosen by WebPlus**. The format of the graphic is as defined in Site properties (Generated Graphics; Default Format); the name is generated automatically, e.g. wp479d0ea6.

    *   **Save in this format with a name chosen by WebPlus**.
        Click a GIF, JPEG, or PNG radio button to specify the export format for the current graphic. Enable **Use site default settings** if the site's default format is to be maintained but named automatically by WebPlus. If selecting JPEG, choose a compression quality from the **Compression** drop-down menu.

    *   **Save to my chosen path and name**.
        Click the **Choose File...** button. The displayed dialog lets you export with the original image file name (enable **Use default name**) or choose a new image name (enable **Choose name** button and enter a new file name). For either method, you can navigate to the folder where you want to save the exported image. The file format used will be that set in the site default settings. You can still override the site default setting by altering the file extension in the Choose name field, e.g. change .GIF to .PNG.

4. Check the **Exclude this picture from optimization..** option if you don't want the image to be combined into one exported image if overlapping with another image in your site.

5. (Optional) Choose from one of several resampling methods—WebPlus can resample when needed, the file will always be resampled (e.g., when a JPG is resized) or will never be resampled (original image will be used). Enable the appropriate radio button as needed. Changing the format will always resample.

6. To enter a title for a graphic, view the ALT and TITLE tab, and enter the appropriate text. This is shown when hovering over an exported image.

7. In the same tab, assign an ALT text string to your image for web accessibility. The string is read out by screen reader on hover over. You can assign text by entry into the input box or you can check **Use default ALT text** instead. For the latter, the image is exported as follows:

    •   If the images is decorative (contains no text) it will have no ALT text.
        OR

    •   If the image is a clickable graphic such as a labeled button (e.g. Back, Forward, etc.), text on the image is automatically taken, exported as ALT text (i.e., Back, Forward) and presented to a screen reader. If a title graphic is specified, the title text is used as the ALT text.

8. Click **OK**.

Importing TWAIN images

If your scanner or digital camera provides **TWAIN** support, you can scan pictures directly into WebPlus using the TWAIN standard, or save the scanned image and then import into WebPlus.

To set up your TWAIN device for importing:

•   See the documentation supplied with your scanner for operating instructions

To import a scanned image:

- Choose **Picture** from the **Insert** menu, then select **TWAIN** then **Acquire...** from the submenus to open a file selection dialog.

If you have more than one TWAIN-compatible device installed, you may need to select which source you wish to scan with.

To select a different TWAIN source for scanning:

1. Choose **Picture** from the **Insert** menu, then select **TWAIN** then **Select Source...** from the submenu.

2. Identify the device you want to use as your TWAIN source.

Applying PhotoLab filters

Filters can be applied and managed in **PhotoLab**, a powerful studio for applying adjustment and effect filters to pictures individually or in combination—all instantly applied and previewed! PhotoLab offers the following key features:

- **Adjustment filters**
  Apply tonal, color, lens, and sharpening filters.

- **Effect filters**
  Apply distortion, blur, stylistic, noise, render, artistic and various other effects.

- **Retouching filters**
  Apply red-eye correction, spot repair, straightening, and cropping.

- **Non-destructive operation**
  All filters are applied without affecting the original picture, and can be edited at any point in the future.

- **Powerful filter combinations**
  Create combinations of mixed adjustment, retouching, and effect filters for savable workflows.

- **Selective masking**
  Apply filters to selected regions using masks.

- **Save and manage favorites**
  Save filter combinations to a handy Favorites tab.

- **Viewing controls**
  Compare before-and-after previews, with dual- and split-screen controls. Use pan and zoom control for moving around your picture.

- **Locking controls**
  Protect your applied filters from accidental change, then optionally apply them to other images on selection.

PhotoLab hosts filter tabs, a main toolbar, and applied filter stack around a central workspace.

main
toolbar

main
workspace

filter
stack

filter
tabs

Images
tab

Pictures present in your publication will show in your **Images tab** if the tab is expanded. This tab is hidden by default in PhotoLab but can be viewed by clicking the ▬▬▲▬▬ button at the bottom of your workspace.

To launch PhotoLab:

1. Select the picture that you want to apply a filter to.

2. Click 🔘 **PhotoLab** on the Picture context toolbar.

Applying a filter

Filters are stored in PhotoLab's Favorites, Adjustments, and Effects tabs which group filters logically into categories (e.g., Quick Fix for fast and commonly used correction filters).

The Favorites tab offers some commonly used filters (individual and in combination).You can complement these with your own user-defined filters.

To apply a filter with trialling:

1. Click a filter thumbnail.

2. As soon as a filter is selected it is temporarily added to **Trial Zone** which lets you experiment freely with your own settings for that filter; the picture automatically refreshes to preview your new settings.

3. Adjust sliders (or enter input values) until your filter suits your requirements. Some filters offer check boxes, drop-down menus, and additional controls (e.g., Advanced settings).

★ Selecting a new filter always replaces the current filter.

Any filter can be temporarily disabled, reset, or deleted from the trial zone.

To disable: Click ▣ , then click ▢ to enable again.

To reset: Click ⟲ . Any changes to settings are reverted back to the filter's defaults.

To delete: Click ❎ .

Once you're sure that you want to keep your filter, you'll need to commit the filter to your filters stack.

To commit your filter:

- Click 🌀 **Commit** to accept your changes. This adds the filter to the right-most **Filters** stack where additional filters can be added and built up by using the same method.

> 🡒 Adjustments are applied such that the most recently added filter always appears at the bottom of the list and is applied to the picture last (after the other filters above it).

To reorder filters:

- Drag and drop your filter into any position in the stack. A dotted line indicates the new position in which the entry will be placed on mouse release.

To add a filter directly (without trialling):

- Click ⚙ **Add Quick Filter** at the top of the Filters stack and choose a filter from the flyout categories. The filter is applied directly to the stack without trialling.

Retouching

PhotoLab offers some useful retouching tools on the main toolbar, each commonly used to correct photos before applying color correction and effects.

Selective masking

Rather than apply a filter to uniformly change the appearance of your picture, you can change only selected regions instead. PhotoLab lets you mask picture areas by painting areas to be either affected by filters or simply left alone.

To apply a mask:

1. From the  **Mask** drop-down menu, select **New Mask**.

2. In the Tool Settings pane, select the ![Add Region icon] **Add Region** tool to allow you to mask regions by painting.

3. Adjust the settings to suit requirements, especially adjusting Brush Size to paint larger or more intricate regions.

✦ Change the **Mode** drop-down menu from Select to Protect to protect painted regions from masking (i.e., the inverse of the Add Region option).

---

4. Using the on-screen cursor, paint regions (in green for adding; red for protecting).

    If you've not been as accurate as you'd like while painting, you can click **Remove Regions** then paint over the unwanted painted regions.

5. Click ☑ to save your masking changes.

💡 The mask button changes to yellow when a mask is applied (i.e., 🎭 ▾).

It's also possible to create additional masks for the same filter as above, and then choose between masks accordingly. You can only have one mask applied at any one time. By using the menu's **New From>** option you can also base the new mask on another mask applied to the current or any other filter in the filter stack. This is useful when using favorites containing multiple adjustments.

To edit a mask:

*   Click the down arrow on the 🎭 ▾ button, choose the mask name and select **Edit Mask**.

Saving favorites

If there's a specific filter setting (or combination of filters) you want to keep for future use it's easy to save it as a **favorite**. PhotoLab stores all your favorites together in the Favorites tab. You can even create your own categories (e.g. My Adjustments) within the tab.

To save filter(s) as a new favorite:

- Click **Save Filter**.

- From the dialog, enter a favorite name and pick a category to save the filter to. (Click [...] to create new category)

If you want to further manage your favorites into user-defined categories, click the option on the ▷ **Tab Menu**.

Exiting PhotoLab

- Click ✔ **Ok**.

Using Image Cutout Studio

Image Cutout Studio offers a powerful integrated solution for cutting objects out from their backgrounds. Depending on the make up of your images you can separate subject of interests from their backgrounds, either by retaining the subject of interest (usually people, objects, etc.) or removing a simple uniform background (e.g., sky, studio backdrop). In both instances, the resulting "cutout" image creates an eye-catching look for your publication.

The latter background removal method is illustrated in the following multi-image example.

The white initial background is discarded, leaving interim checkerboard transparency, from which another image can be used as a more attractive background. A red tint on the second image's background is used to indicate areas to be discarded.

To launch Image Cutout Studio:

1. Select an image to be cut out.

2. Select ![icon] **Image Cutout Studio** from the displayed Picture context toolbar. Image Cutout Studio is launched.

Choose an output

It's essential that you choose an output type prior to selecting areas for keeping/discarding. Either an alpha-edged or vector-cropped bitmap can be chosen as your output type prior to selection. The choice you make really depends on the image, in particular how well defined image edges are.

Zoom into your image to examine its edges; this may influence the output type chosen.

Let's look at the output types and explain the difference between each.

Output Type	Description and use
Alpha-edged Bitmap	Use when cutting out objects with poorly defined edges. Transparency and pixel blending are used at the outline edge to produce professional results with negligible interference from background colors. The term "alpha" refers to a 32-bit image's alpha transparency channel.
Vector-cropped Bitmap	Use on more well-defined edges. A cropped image with crop outline is created which can be later manipulated with the crop tools. You can optionally apply feathering to the image edge but will not remove background color.

To create an alpha-edged bitmap:

1. Select **Alpha-edged Bitmap** from the **Output Type** drop-down menu.

2. (Optional) Drag the **Width** slider to set the extent to which the "alpha" blending is applied inside the cutout edge.

3. (Optional) Adjust the **Blur** slider to smooth out the cutout edge.

To create a vector-cropped bitmap:

1. Select **Vector-cropped Bitmap** from the **Output Type** drop-down menu.

2. (Optional) Drag the **Feather** slider to apply a soft or blurry edge inside the cutout edge.

3. (Optional) Drag the **Smoothness** slider to smooth out the cutout edge.

4. (Optional) The **Inflate** slider acts as a positive or negative offset from the cutout edge.

Selecting areas to keep or discard

A pair of brushes for keeping and discarding is used to "paint" areas of the image. The tools are called **Keep Brush** and **Discard Brush**, and are either used independently or, more typically, in combination with each other. When using either tool, the brush paints an area contained by an outline which is considered to be discarded or retained (depending on brush type). A configurable number of pixels adjacent to the outline area are blended.

To aid the selection operation, several display modes are available to show selection.

Show Original, **Show Tinted**, and **Show Transparent** buttons respectively display the image with:

- selection areas only

- various colored tints aiding complex selection operations

- checkerboard transparency areas marked for discarding.

For Show tinted, a red tint indicates areas to be discarded; a green tint shows areas to be kept.

Background Color

For Show transparent mode, a different **Background color** can be set (at bottom of the Studio) which might help differentiate areas to keep or discard.

To select image areas for keeping/discarding:

1. In Image Cutout Studio, click either [icon] **Keep brush** or [icon] **Discard brush** from the left of the Studio workspace.

2. (Optional) Pick a **Brush size** suitable for the area to be worked on.

3. (Optional) Set a **Grow tolerance** value to automatically expand the selected area under the cursor (by detecting colors similar to those within the current selection). The greater the value the more the selected area will grow.

4. Using the circular cursor, click and drag across the area to be retained. It's OK to repeatedly click and drag until your selection area is made.

The ![Undo icon] **Undo** button reverts to the last made selection.

5. If you're outputting an alpha-edged bitmap, you can refine the area to be kept/discarded within Image Cutout Studio (only after previewing) with Erase and Restore touch-up tools. Vector-cropped images can be cropped using standard WebPlus crop tools outside of the Studio.

> Make your outline edge as exact as possible by using brush and touch-up tools before committing your work.

6. Click ![OK icon] **OK** to create your cutout, or click ![Cancel icon] **Cancel**.

You'll see your image on the poster page in its original location, but with the selected areas cut away (made transparent).

> Click ![Reset icon] **Reset** if you want to revert your selected areas and start your cutout again.

Refining your cutout area (alpha-edged bitmaps only)

If a vector-cropped image is created via Image Cutout Studio it's possible to subsequently manipulate the crop outline using crop tools. However, for alpha-edged bitmaps, Erase and Restore touch-up tools can be used to refine the cutout area within the Studio before completing your cutout. The latter can't be edited with crop tools.

> The touch-up tools are brush based and are only to be used to fine-tune your almost complete cutout—use your Keep and Discard brush tools for the bulk of your work!

To restore or remove portions of your cutout:

1. With your cutout areas already defined, click ⊙ **Preview** (Output settings tab). You can use the button to check your cutout as you progress.

2. Click the ▨ **Restore Touch-up Tool** or ▨ **Erase Touch-up Tool** button from the left of the Studio workspace.

3. Paint the areas for restoring or erasing as you would with the brush tools.

4. Click ⊘ **Ok**.

> ★ If you've touched up part of your image between each preview, you'll be asked if you want to save or discard changes.

Adding animation

WebPlus lets you add several varieties of eye-catching animation effects to any web page: **animated marquees**, **GIF animations** (See online Help), and **Flash** (.SWF) files. For any of the animation effects, you can preview the animation and/or customize the effect. Once placed into your site, the animations appear static, but they will spring to life once the site has been exported and a visitor views your page in a web browser.

Animated marquees

Animated marquees are an impressive way to add horizontally scrolling motion to a headline or catch phrase. You can choose the background color, enter from one to three lines of text, define text properties (choose from any installed font), scroll direction, speed and alignment for each line. If you like, you can define any link destination type for the marquee (see Adding hyperlinks and anchors on p. 223). For the most compelling effect, select two lines with strongly contrasting text colors and opposing scroll directions.

Animated marquees appear as static graphics on the WebPlus page. You can cut, copy, move, and resize them just like other graphics. They will animate when previewed or viewed in a web browser.

To create an animated marquee:

- Click the **Insert Animated Marquee** button on the **Web Objects** toolbar's Media flyout.

To edit an animated marquee you've already defined:

- Double-click the marquee. The Insert Animated Marquee dialog redisplays, with the current settings in place.

Flash files

A Flash (*.SWF) file is a viewable movie using the Flash™ Player format. (Flash is a vector-based program designed to create and display small files on the web.) Flash files can be added to your page (much like an image) and will play within your page view without the need for previewing in your browser (or WebPlus preview window). You can cut, copy, move, and resize them just like other graphics.

To see some Flash files in action, the Gallery tab hosts a stunning collection of Flash banners (each with pre-assigned Flash parameters already set) which can be easily adopted. These banners are designed to allow you to customize their appearance (i.e., text, images, and scheme colors) without any prior Flash design experience.

To insert a Flash file:

1. Click the **Insert Flash file** button on the **Web Objects** toolbar's Media flyout.

2. Use the dialog to select the Flash file to open (click **Browse...** then select your .SWF file). Click **Export Options** to optionally define a different file name and/or file location. To keep the animation separate from the WebPlus file (using a link to the source file) uncheck **Embed files in site**.

3. (Optional) In the **Parameters** window, click the **Add...** (or **Edit**) button to add parameters as name/value pairs.

4. (Optional) In the **Additional Files** window, build up a library of files (e.g., images) which are used to make up your Flash movie. Think of it as a local library in which supporting files are easily at hand and

easily referenced. Click the **Add...** button to navigate to then select files for addition (use Ctrl-click or Shift-click for contiguous or non-contiguous file selection, respectively).

5. (Optional) The Display box controls how the Flash movie is presented on your WebPlus page. Experiment with the options for different looping, transparency, alignment, scaling, and quality options.

6. Click **OK**.

7. You'll see the ⊞ Picture Paste cursor. Click to insert the file at a default size or drag to set a custom size region.

To edit a Flash banner:

1. Double-click your Flash movie.

2. (Optional) Change **Export Options...** and whether you want to embed the file in your WebPlus site.

3. In the Parameters box select any parameter **Name** in the list and click the **Edit** button (you don't need to use the **Add...** button when editing Flash banners). Depending on the Flash banner chosen, you can edit several types of parameter value, i.e.

*   Text values can be changed from their placeholder text, e.g. a placeholder text value for "line 1" can be overwritten with your own text (e.g., "Say it.."). You can equally use a token as a replacement value (e.g. a token of *%companyname%* will

automatically show the company name set in User Details in your banner—in this case "Flowers-2-Go").

- Scheme values can be altered by again editing token values, e.g. to use your site's scheme color 2 instead or scheme color 1 you can edit %scheme1% to be %scheme2%.

- Parameter values for pictures work slight differently to text and schemes. Flash banners are arranged in the Gallery tab in folders representing the number of pictures used in the banner design, i.e. "1 Image", "2 Image" and "3 Image". Each picture that makes up your banner is referenced in the parameters list, e.g. for "3 Image" banners, Pic1URL, Pic2URL, and Pic3URL represents the first, second and third pictures listed in the **Additional Files** list. You can either reorder pictures in the Additional Files list (**not** the Parameters list) using the **Up** or **Down** buttons to make pictures appear in a different sequence or use the right-most **Add...** button to add new files to the Additional Files list to replace currently referenced pictures. There's no need to edit the Parameter values at all—the key is to set the pictures and their order in the Additional Files list only.

> ★ Remember to remove any unwanted pictures from the Additional Files list.

4. (Optional) Uncheck **Embed files in site** if you don't want additional files to be included in your site.

5. (Optional) The Display box controls how the Flash movie is presented on your WebPlus page. Experiment with the options for different looping, transparency, alignment, scaling, and quality options.

6. Click **OK**.

The selected Flash banner is shown with any previously made edits applied.

> ★ If you experience any playback problems when Flash files are placed on your page, it is possible to uncheck **Load Flash previews** in **Tools>Options** (Layout menu option). Exported web pages containing Flash files are unaffected.

Adding sound and video

WebPlus lets you augment your web pages with sound and video files in a variety of standard formats, including both **non-streaming** and **streaming** media. In addition, WebPlus lets you include third-party videos already hosted on **www.youtube.com**.

Sound

- There are actually two sound playback options—**background sound**, where a sound loads and plays automatically when a specific page is first displayed in the visitor's web browser, and **linked sound**, triggered by a mouse click (for example on an icon or hyperlinked object). The supported audio formats are .AIFF, .AU, MIDI (.mid, .midi), .MP3, RealAudio (.ra, .ram), and .WAV.

Video

- **Linked video** works like linked sound. Supported video formats are .AVI, QuickTime (.mov, .qt), MPEG (.mpg, .mpeg, .mpe, .mpv), and RealVideo (.ram, .rv). (Non-streaming files must download in entirety to a user's computer before they begin playing; streaming files require a special player that buffers incoming data and can start playing before the whole clip has arrived.)

- **YouTube videos** which are already published on the Internet can be included on your web page. Videos themselves are not be embedded in your site; instead, just the unique YouTube video ID is embedded in your page as you place the YouTube video on your page—a link is created from your web page back to **www.youtube.com**. This lets you add media content to your pages while avoiding uploading large videos as part of your site.

With both background and linked sound (or video), you have the option of **embedding** the source file in your site, as opposed to keeping it separate (remember that YouTube videos cannot be embedded in your site). Although embedding any file adds to the size of the site, it is the default option because you'll no longer have to worry about juggling separate files or the chance of accidentally deleting one of them. When you publish your site, WebPlus takes care of exporting and copying both embedded and non-embedded files.

To add background sound to a page:

1. Right-click the page in the workspace and choose **Page Properties...**.

2. From the **Effects** tab, check **Use sound file**, then from the Open dialog, browse to the sound file you want to add. Once the file is selected, click **OK**.

3. If you do **not** wish to embed the file, uncheck the **Embed sound file in site** option.

4. To have the sound play back as a continuous loop, check **Loop sound**. Otherwise, it will play just once.

5. (Optional) Set **Export Options...** to define an exported file name and physical location. (See Setting image export options on p. 177.)

6. Click **OK**.

The sound file will download and play back when the web page displays in a browser.

The basic question is how you want the visitor to be able to trigger the playback of a given media file. WebPlus offers the same basic options for both kinds of media:

-   **From a hyperlinked object (or hotspot):** You start with an existing object in the site, and hyperlink it to the media file, or use a hotspot over an image.

-   **From a video thumbnail preview**: You click on an embedded video thumbnail which commences video playback (YouTube videos only).

-   **From an icon:** WebPlus provides an icon pre-linked to the media file. You then position the icon on your page.

-   **From a picture:** You select an external picture file, which WebPlus then imports and links to the media file.

- **Inline:** A media "player" will be visible on your published web page (rather than appearing after the user clicks a link, icon, or picture). In WebPlus, you'll see a marker on the page where the player will appear.

With the first two options, the media file remains external and can't be embedded in your site. Options 3 to 5 give you the choice of embedding the media file.

To add linked sound or video to an object or hotspot:

1. Select the object or hotspot and choose **Hyperlink** from the **Tools** toolbar.

2. In the dialog, select **File** to create a hyperlink to a sound file on your hard disk.

3. Click **Browse**, locate and select the media file, and click **Open**.

4. If you do **not** wish to embed the file, uncheck the **Embed picture file in site** option.

5. (Optional) Set **Export Options...** to define an exported file name and physical location. (See Setting image export options on p. 177.)

6. A range of target windows can be chosen depending on how you want the link destination to be displayed. (See Adding hyperlinks and anchors on p. 223.).

7. Click **Ok**.

To embed a YouTube video:

1. Open the **www.youtube.com** website in your browser, and choose the YouTube video that you want to link to.

2. Copy the URL address for the video (or embed code). This contains an alphanumeric ID, e.g. ySnp4YXU6JQ, which uniquely identifies the video clip.

3. Click the **Insert YouTube Video** button on the **Web Objects** toolbar's Media flyout.
   OR

Choose **Media** from the **Insert** menu and select **YouTube Video...** from the submenu.

4.   From the dialog, paste the video URL into the input box.

5.   (Optional) Check/Uncheck the boxes to enable/disable the following;

   •   **Autoplay**
       Automatically plays the video once the page has loaded.

   •   **Loop**
       Continuously plays the video.

   •   **Show video info**
       Displays the title and star rating of the video.

   •   **Allow full screen mode**
       Adds a button to the video window so that the user can opt to view the video in full screen mode.

   •   **Include related videos**
       (If **Loop** is checked, the **Include related videos** feature is automatically disabled. If you want to enable this feature, you will need to clear the Loop check box.) At the end of the video, displays recommended videos related in content to the current video playing on your page. Also displays a search bar so that users can browse and play other videos from YouTube on your site.

   •   **Play in HD**
       Plays the video in High-Definition, if the video itself has been created for High-Definition playback.

   •   **Show Border**
       Adds a border around the video window. Click the two buttons to access drop-down palettes and select up to two colors.

6.   Click **OK**. Position the ▦ **Paste** cursor where you want the top-left corner of your video to be placed.

7. To insert the video at a default size, simply click the mouse.
   OR
   To set the size of the inserted video, drag out the cursor and release the mouse button. The video resizing will be unconstrained but you can maintain the video's aspect ratio by pressing the **Shift** key as you drag.

Some websites may require their YouTube video(s) to be swapped for another on an occasional or more regular basis. For example, the site may host a regularly changing top 10 or videos with topical content. Either way, WebPlus can replace videos without affecting their placement.

To swap your YouTube video for another, double-click an existing YouTube video. From the dialog, paste a previously copied video URL into the input box.

To link from an icon, picture, or inline player:

1. Click the 🎵 **Insert Sound Clip** or 🎬 **Insert Video Clip** button on the **Web Objects** toolbar's Media flyout.

2. Browse to locate the media file name.

3. Select a link display option (icon, inline, or picture).

4. If you do **not** wish to embed the file, uncheck the **Embed picture file in site** option.

5. Click **OK** to close the dialog, then click (or click and drag) with the cursor to place the icon, picture, or marker on your page.

Using the Photo Gallery

The simultaneous expansion of digital camera usage and Broadband services has created a fantastic opportunity for publishing photo collections on web pages. There are a multitude of reasons for doing so but some common ones include:

- hosting family photos for access by geographically distant relatives

- Special occasions (parties, Christmas, meetings, holidays)

- cataloguing collections (e.g., of animals, stamps, etc.)

In WebPlus you can add a Flash™- or JavaScript-based photo gallery to any web page. By using the power of Flash you can also adopt some eye-catching gallery styles, each offering different ways of cycling through photos. Photo galleries let you navigate via a top or bottom control bar or, depending on gallery style, by using:

- thumbnail rollovers (opposite)

- vertical thumbnails

- photo grids

- photo stacks

Photos can be imported by file or folder, or from a TWAIN device (digital camera/scanner). By default, large photos imported into the gallery are automatically resized and exported at the maximum resolution of 720 x 540 pixels. If photos are smaller than 720 x 540 pixels, they will remain unchanged.

During import, you have the option to manage multiple selected photos simultaneously.

- Reorder your photos into your preferred display order.

- Perform bulk editing. You'll be able to caption, rotate*, and adjust brightness, and contrast.

- Assign Exif tags and create custom captions.

*Automatic rotation of digital camera photos (landscape to portrait) is possible (if supported by camera)

Creating the Gallery

The Photo Gallery is inserted on the page, just like an individual photo, after collecting your photos together from file, folder, camera, or scanner.

> ★ All the photos are output as JPGs regardless of the original photo type and the settings in **File>Site Properties>Graphics**.

To insert a Photo Gallery:

1. Click the ▣ **Insert Photo Gallery** button on the **Standard Objects** toolbar's Picture flyout.

2. (Optional) Click **Advanced** to change default photo size and quality settings.

3. Select the type of photo gallery you want to use;

    *   **Flash Photo Gallery**
        (Visitors to your site will require Flash 8 and above.)

    *   **JavaScript Photo Gallery**

4. Click **Next**. From the dialog, choose whether to:

    *   **Add individual files**
        Click the **Add Files** button to navigate to then select the photo file(s) to open. Use **Ctrl**-click or **Shift**-click to select multiple non-adjacent or adjacent files. Use the **Preview** window to examine the photos as you add to your current selection.

        OR

    *   **Add all photos in a folder**
        Click the **Add Folder** button to navigate to a folder then select it to add its contents.

        OR

    *   **Add from a digital camera or scanner**
        Click the **Add TWAIN** button. If needed, select your TWAIN source in advance of the acquisition process via **Select Source...**

from the drop-down menu. You can also specify a folder in which to save the photos to once they have been acquired via **Set Export Folder...** from the drop-down menu. Click **Acquire...** to get your photos.

- To delete one or all thumbnails, select and click the **Delete** button.

Your photos display as thumbnails in the **Photo Gallery** dialog.

5. (Optional) Select one or more gallery thumbnails for manipulation;

- To adjust photo order, use the ⬆ **Up** and ⬇ **Down** buttons at the bottom of the dialog.
  OR

  Click 📥 **Move to position** and input a position number.

- To rotate in 90° clockwise intervals, click the 🔄 **Rotate** button.
  OR
  Click the **Rotate right** column and select a rotation increment from the drop-down.

- To add a caption, click the **Caption** column and input text, numbers and characters.

- ⬄ To create captions from Exif, IPTC and XMP photo tags, click **Format Captions**. Select a tag type from the drop-down and then click **Add Tag**. A preview will display in the **Caption Preview** box. Select how to add the captions to any existing ones—**Add to start of caption**, **Add to end of caption** or **Overwrite caption**. Click **Ok**.

- To find and replace captions, click 🔍 **Find caption**. (See the topic Using find and replace on p. 92.)

- To adjust **Brightness** and **Contrast**, click the respective columns and input values between 0 and 100.

- To replace a photo, right-click the selected photo and then click **Replace image**.

6. To include selected photos within your site, check **Embed Images**. By default, photos are kept separate from the WebPlus file (using a link to the source file).

7. Click **Next**.

8. Select a Gallery style from the **Gallery Style** pane running across the top of the dialog. Each type offers a different style for photo navigation—try each one out until you find one you like in the accompanying Preview window. You'll notice a control bar on each style which allows for user navigation of photos after publishing.

9. (Optional) For the selected style, use the pane on the right to modify various gallery-wide options (accompanying background music, font color, AutoPlay, etc.). Some options are specific to a gallery style such as enabling/disabling thumbnail rollovers, number of thumbnails shown, photos per stack, etc. Blur amount controls how much blurring occurs between photos. AutoPlay will automatically start photo display at a set but configurable time interval (in seconds). Otherwise, the control bar shown on the photo gallery after publishing can initiate photo playback.

10. Click **Finish**.

11. To insert the gallery at a default size, position the displayed cursor where you want the gallery to appear on the page, then simply click the mouse.
OR
To set the size of the inserted gallery, drag out a region and release the mouse button.

Editing the Photo Gallery

Once added to the web page, the Photo Gallery can be edited. Photos can be added, removed, rotated, captioned, or adjusted via PhotoLab. You can also swap your existing gallery style for another, change background music, caption text color, and set your gallery to autoplay (photos will automatically cycle).

To edit a Photo Gallery:

1. Select a gallery already present on your web page.

2. Double-click the gallery.

The Photo Gallery dialog is displayed. The options available are the same as those available when the gallery was created.

> Once a Flash gallery is placed on the page it's also possible to drag a corner of the gallery object to resize. Use the **Ctrl** key while dragging to maintain the aspect ratio.

Linking remote images

It is possible to connect to any image currently available on the Internet. However, to prevent copyright infringement it's advisable to use images from a reliable image hosting service. Of course you may be able to "hotlink" to other images (from a friend or colleague's site) where legal implications are not an issue but it's only polite to **ask for permission first**!

To insert a remote image:

1. Go to **Insert>Picture>Remote link...**.

2. In the dialog, enter the absolute URL for the image.

3. Click **OK**.

4. You'll see the mouse pointer change to the ⊞ Picture Paste cursor. What you do next determines the initial size and placement of the image.

5. To insert the image at a default size, simply click the mouse.
    OR
    To set the size of the inserted image, drag out a region and release the mouse button.

10 Color, Fills, and Transparency

Applying solid colors

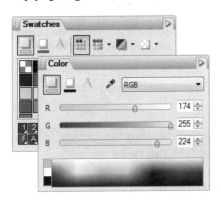

You can use the Color tab, Swatches tab or a dialog box to apply solid colors to an object.

The tabs' swatch buttons offer a number of ways to apply solid colors to objects of different kinds:

- You can apply solid colors to an object's **fill** or **line**. As you might expect, QuickShapes and closed shapes (see Drawing and editing shapes on p. 148) have both line and fill properties.

- **Freehand** or **curved lines** can take **line** colors but also a **fill** color for creating closed shapes directly from the line.

- Selected **artistic** and **Creative frame text objects** can take a background fill, line, and a text color. The text color is the fill of the text, the background fill is the area immediately behind the text. HTML frame text only takes a background fill and text color.

- **Text frames** (shown) and **table cells** can have a background fill independent of the characters they contain.

To apply a solid color via the Color tab:

1. Select the object(s) or highlight a range of text.

2. Click the **Color** tab and select one of several color modes (RGB, CMYK, or HSL) from the drop-down list.

3. Click the ⬜ **Fill** or ⬜ **Line**, or **A** **Text** button at the top of the tab to determine where color will be applied. The color of the underline reflects the color of your selected object. For selected frame text, the Fill will be the background text color (but not the frame's background color).

4. Select a color from the color spectrum or sliders depending on color mode selected.

> In RGB color mode, you can use hexadecimal color coding by selection from the Color tab's ▷ **Tab Menu** button.

To apply a solid color via the Swatches tab:

1. Select the object(s) or highlight a range of text.

2. Click the **Swatches** tab.

3. Click the ⬜ **Fill** or ⬜ **Line**, or **A** **Text** button at the top of the tab to determine where color will be applied.

4. Select a color swatch from the **Publication Palette** (commonly used colors and those previously applied in your site) or standard **Palette** (standard RGB or themed palette presets such as WebSafe colors).

Alternatively, use **Format>Fill...** to apply color via a dialog.

To change a solid color's shade/tint (lightness):

1. Select the object and set the correct Fill, Line or Text button in the Color tab.

2. From the Color mode drop-down menu, select **Tinting**.

3. Drag the Shade/Tint slider to the left or right to darken or lighten your starting color, respectively. You can also enter a percentage value in the box (entering 0 in the input box reverts to the original color).

Object tinting can also be applied via the Swatches tab—adjust | 0% ▶ | **Tint** via slider or direct input.

WebPlus automatically adds used colors to the 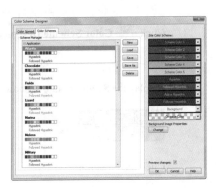 Publication Palette in the Swatches tab.

To change the current palette:

- Click the **Palette** button to view and adopt colors from a standard RGB, WebSafe, or selection of themed palettes. Colors can be added, edited or deleted from the Publication Palette but not from other palettes.

Using color schemes

WebPlus offers an impressive selection of **color schemes** that can be selected when creating a site using a design template. If you choose a template-based site, the selection of a color scheme will set the look and feel of your site with respect to color, as all templates are already "schemed."

Websites created from a template can either use one of three color schemes designed specifically for that template design, or just use global color schemes. Websites created from scratch use globally available color schemes—you can still use any color scheme but you'll have to assign scheme color to objects as they are created. This will allow dramatic color change if you subsequently change schemes.

The color scheme can be changed at any time by using the **Color Scheme Designer**, which also lets you modify scheme colors and even create your own custom color schemes.

Schemes that have been modified are stored with the site, although custom color schemes can also be saved globally, so the full set of schemes is always available to new sites.

How color schemes work

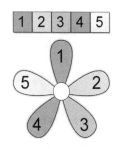

Color schemes in WebPlus work much like a paint-by-numbers system, where various regions of a layout are coded with numbers, and a specific **basic color** is assigned (by number) to each region. For example, consider the petal opposite, labelled with the numbers 1 through 5. To fill it in, you'd use paint from the paint jars numbered 1 through 5. Swapping different colors into the paint jars, while keeping the numbers on the drawing the same, would produce a differently colored petal **automatically**.

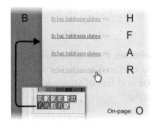

Each scheme also includes **adjunct colors** which apply specifically to hyperlinks (default **H**, followed **F**, active **A**, rollover **R**), off-page window backgrounds (**B**), and on-page colors (**O**).

Each site can have just one color scheme active at any one time; this is called the **site color scheme** and is always shown in the Swatches tab. When you save a site, its current color scheme is saved along with the site.

To select a preset color scheme:

1. Click  **Color Scheme Designer** on the default context toolbar.

   OR

   Display the **Swatches** tab, to show the current color scheme, e.g.

   Click the ·· button.

2. From the dialog's Color Schemes tab, double-click a different color scheme sample from the list (or select and click **Load**), then click **OK**. Any regions in the site that have been assigned one of the five color scheme numbers are updated with the corresponding color from the new scheme; adjunct colors are also updated.

You can repeat this selection process indefinitely.

Adjunct colors

As well the five basic scheme colors, each scheme includes six **adjunct colors** which control color in response to user hyperlink interactivity; the color of page and off-page (window) backgrounds are also affected.

These can be modified as for scheme colors 1-5, with Background color/image and On-Page color being exceptions.

- The **Hyperlink** color (labeled **H**) applies to hyperlinked text **before** it's been clicked on.

- The **Followed Hyperlink** color (labeled **F**), applies to hyperlinked text after a visitor has clicked to "follow" the link.

- The **Active Hyperlink** color (labeled **A**), applies to hyperlinked text when a visitor's mouse button is depressed. Typically this is the color shown after clicking and before the hyperlink's page is displayed.

- The **Rollover** color (labeled **R**), applies to hyperlinked text when a visitor's mouse button rolls over it.

- The **Background** (labeled **B**) applies to either an off-page background color or picture shown outside your web page if the user resizes the browser's window to be larger than the web page dimensions.

- The **On-page** color (labeled **O**), is used to fill the page's background. If you make this transparent, the currently set underlying background shows, making the page boundaries invisible (content is still constrained to page dimensions).

Applying scheme colors to objects

If you create new objects in a web template site, or start a site from scratch, how can you extend a color scheme to the new objects? Although you'll need to spend some time working out which color combinations look best, the mechanics of the process are simple. Recalling the paint-by-numbers example above, all you need to do is assign one of the five scheme color numbers to an object's line and/or fill.

To assign a scheme color to an object:

1. Select the object and choose a **Fill**, **Line**, or **Text** button at the top of the Swatches tab depending on the desired effect.

2. From the bottom of the Swatches tab, click on a scheme color (numbered 1 to 5) that you want to apply to the fill, line and text (or you can drag the color instead).

If an object's fill uses a scheme color, the corresponding sample in Swatches tab will be highlighted whenever the object is selected.

Modifying color schemes

If you've tried various color schemes but haven't found one that's quite right, you can modify any of the colors in an existing scheme.

To modify a color scheme:

1. Click **Color Scheme Designer** on the default context toolbar.

2. From the Color Schemes tab, select the scheme to modify (double-click a scheme or select and click **Load**).

3. From the dialog, each of the five scheme color numbers (plus the adjunct colors) has its own drop-down menu, showing available colors in the WebPlus palette.

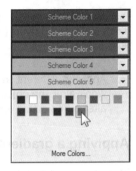

Click the scheme color's drop-down arrow and select a color from the menu (or click **More Colors...** for more color choice).

The scheme is updated with the new color. Repeat to modify other scheme colors.

4. To apply the scheme to the current site, click **OK**. The site color scheme is now updated.

> 💡 From the **Change** button, you can select a "schemed" picture for use as the off-page browser window background.

> ★ To create a new named scheme based on these colors, click **Save As...**. Alternatively, use **Save** to overwrite the existing scheme.

For more advanced color scheme design using suggested color combinations, see online Help.

Working with gradient and bitmap fills

Gradient fills provide a gradation or spectrum of colors spreading between two or more points on an object. A gradient fill has an editable path with nodes that mark the origin of each of these key colors. A bitmap fill uses a named bitmap—often a material, pattern, or background image—to fill an object.

Linear   *Elliptical*   *Conical*   *Bitmap*

You can apply preset gradient and bitmap fills from the Swatches tab to shapes, text frames, table cells, and to any artistic, creative frame, and creative table text (but not to HTML frame text or HTML table text). Using the **Fill Tool** from the **Tools** toolbar's Fill flyout (or from **Format>Fill**), you can vary the fill's path on an object for different effects (see online Help).

> ★ Applying different transparency effects (using the Transparency tab) won't alter the object's fill settings as such, but may significantly alter a fill's actual appearance.

Applying a gradient or bitmap fill

There are several ways to apply a gradient or bitmap fill: using the Swatches tab, Fill Tool, or a dialog.

The easiest way to apply a gradient or bitmap fill is to use one of a range of pre-supplied swatch thumbnails in the Swatches tab's **Gradient** or **Bitmap** palettes. The Fill Tool and a Fill dialog are alternative methods for creating gradient fills (these are covered in online Help).

To apply a gradient or bitmap fill using the Swatches tab:

1. Click the Swatches tab and ensure the ▣ **Fill** button is selected. Note that the color of the underline reflects the color of your selected object.

2. 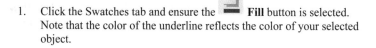 For gradient fills, select Linear, Elliptical or Conical as the gradient type from the **Gradient** button's drop-down menu.
    OR
    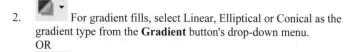 For bitmap fills, select a drop-down menu category from the **Bitmap** button.

3. Select the object(s), and click the appropriate gallery swatch for the fill you want to apply.
    OR
    Drag from the gallery swatch onto any object and release the mouse button.

4. If needed, adjust the fill's **Tint** at the bottom of the tab with the tab slider or set a percentage value in the input box.

See Updating and saving defaults on p. 137 for more details.

Setting transparency

Transparency effects are great for highlights, shading and shadows, and simulating "rendered" realism. They can make the critical difference between flat-looking illustrations and images with depth and snap. WebPlus fully supports variable transparency and lets you apply solid, gradient, or bitmap transparencies easily.

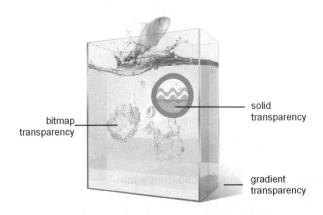

Transparencies work rather like fills that use "disappearing ink" instead of color. The more transparency in a particular spot, the more "disappearing" takes place there, and the more the object(s) underneath show through. Just as a gradient fill can vary from light to dark, a transparency can vary from more to less, i.e. from clear to opaque, as in the illustration:

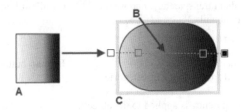

(A) Linear Transparency; (B) Fill path; (C) Effect on graphic

In WebPlus, transparency effects work very much like grayscale fills. Just like fills...

- Transparency effects are applied from the Studio—in this case, using the Transparency tab via solid, gradient, and bitmap galleries.

- The Transparency tab's gallery has thumbnails in shades of gray, where the lighter portions represent more transparency. To apply transparency, you click thumbnails or drag them onto objects.

- Most transparency effects have a path you can edit—in this case, with the Transparency Tool.

Applying transparency

You can apply gradient and bitmap transparency from the Transparency tab to shapes, text frames, table cells, and to any artistic, creative frame, and creative table text (but not to HTML frame text or HTML table text).

To apply transparency with Transparency tab:

1. With your object selected, go to the Transparency tab.

2. For solid transparency, select the 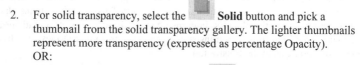 **Solid** button and pick a thumbnail from the solid transparency gallery. The lighter thumbnails represent more transparency (expressed as percentage Opacity).
   OR:

   For gradient transparency, choose the **Gradient** button and pick your thumbnail.
   OR:

   For bitmap transparency, choose the **Bitmap** button and pick a thumbnail from a range of categories.

3. The transparency is applied to the object(s).

Alternatively, drag the desired thumbnail from the gallery to an object, and release the mouse button.

To apply gradient transparency with Transparency Tool:

1. Select a colored object.

2. Click the **Transparency Tool** button on the **Tools** toolbar's Transparency flyout.
    OR
    Select **Format>Transparency....**

3. Drag your cursor across the object and release the mouse button. The object takes a simple Linear transparency, grading from 100% opacity to 0% opacity (fully transparent).

Setting the default transparency

The **default transparency** means the transparency that will be applied to the next new object you create. Local defaults only affect objects in the current site. For information on setting defaults in WebPlus, see Updating and saving defaults on p. 137.

11   Adding Hyperlinks and Interactivity

Adding hyperlinks and anchors

Hyperlinking an object such as a box, some text, or a picture means that a visitor to your website can click on the object to trigger an event. The event is most commonly a jump to one of the following:

- site page

- Internet page (somewhere on the web)

- Email composition window

- File on your local disk or network

- Anchor (a designated target within a web page)

- Smart object (specifically a forum or blog in Serif Web Resources)

- RSS feed or podcast

- Shopping cart

- Navigation bar

- User Data

- Picture

Well-designed hyperlinks are an important aspect of site structure. They help visitors navigate through your site and serve as an important adjunct to logical page relationships as shown in the Site Structure tree. (But don't overlook the time-saving advantages of using navigation bars.)

> You can manage all hyperlinks and anchors throughout your site by using the **Site Manager**, accessible from the Default context toolbar or Hintline.

To add a hyperlink:

1. Use the **Pointer Tool** to select the single or grouped object or highlight the region of text to be hyperlinked.

2. Click the ![icon] **Hyperlink** button on the **Tools** toolbar. The Hyperlinks dialog appears.

3. Click to select the link destination type, and enter the specific hyperlink target, i.e. a site page, internet page, Smart object, email address, etc.

4. Depending on the link type, choose type-specific options

5. A range of target windows or frames can be chosen depending on how you want the link destination to be displayed. The types (along with expected results) are:

    *   **Same Window**: the link destination is shown in the same window from which the hyperlink was clicked.

    *   **New Window**: A new window is used to display the link destination whose properties (dimensions, position, or navigation bar usage) can be defined via the **Settings...** button. The original window will remain open.

    *   **Top of Current Window**: the link destination is shown in the top level window.

    *   **Named Window**: A custom window can be defined by entering a new window name in the right-most drop-down menu. Its properties (dimensions, position, and appearance) can be defined via the **Settings...** button (check **Use JavaScript popup code** first). You can also adopt an existing named window from the same drop-down menu.

6. Choose other properties such as Title name (text displayed on-screen on hover over) and a shortcut access key.
    Note: As a visual cue, hyperlinked words are normally underlined and appear in the color you've specified for Hyperlinks in the Color Scheme Designer or elsewhere (see Using color schemes on p. 211).

7. Click **OK**.

To modify or remove a hyperlink:

1. Use the **Pointer Tool** to select the object, or click for an insertion point inside the linked text. (It's not necessary to drag over a hyperlinked region of text.)

2. Click the **Hyperlink** button on the **Tools** toolbar's Hyperlink flyout.

The Hyperlinks dialog appears with the current link target shown. If the link is in text, the whole text link highlights.

-   To modify the hyperlink, select a new link destination type, target, and/or options.

-   To remove the hyperlink, click **No Hyperlink**.

To view or edit existing hyperlinks:

-   Choose **Site Manager>Hyperlink Manager...** on the **Tools** menu to view, rename, or remove hyperlinks.

Inserting an anchor

An anchor is a specific location on a page that can serve as the target for a hyperlink. Invisible to the web page visitor, it typically marks a point within some text (such as the start of a particular section) or an image at some point down the page. Anchors are useful if your page has enough content to be divided into sections, but not enough to require carving up into separate pages. These let the reader jump to related content without leaving the current page. In the same way, keeping web visitors on the same page makes it less likely they'll get "lost' while perusing the information on your site.

To insert an anchor:

1. Use the **Pointer Tool** to select the target object, or click for an insertion point inside the target text.

2. Click the **Anchor** button on the **Tools** toolbar's Hyperlink flyout.
    OR
    Choose **Anchor...** from the **Insert** or right-click menu.

3. In the dialog, type a name for the anchor.

4. (Optional) Check **Include Anchor in Navigation** to allow the anchor (typically a selected object) to be accessed via a navigation bar instead of a hyperlink. You'll need to check **Include anchors** on your navigation bar first. Give the anchor a title.

    *   Check **Before** and/or **After** to apply horizontal separator lines above/below the anchor as a submenu item in navigation bars.

    *   Add a **Description** to add extra page-related text information on the bar's submenu item.

5. Click **Remove** to delete the anchor intelligently, i.e., you can control what happens to any referencing hyperlinks (i.e., ignore, delete, or redirect).

6. Click **OK**.

Anchors are page-specific, so it's OK to use the same anchor name on more than one page. WebPlus will create anchor names automatically in series for each page, and using prefixes for each type of object. However, you may find it easier to keep track of anchors throughout the site if you supply your own unique names—it's up to you.

To view or edit existing anchors:

*   Choose **Site Manager>Anchor Manager...** on the **Tools** menu to view, rename, or remove an anchor attached to a particular object. You can also include the anchor in page navigation.

Adding hotspots to a page

A hotspot is a transparent hyperlink region on a web page. Usually placed on top of graphics, hotspots act like "buttons" that respond when clicked in a web browser. They are especially useful if you want the visitor to be able to click on different parts of a picture (such as a graphic "menu" or map of your site). You can draw and edit hotspots by hand, or create them to match an existing shape.

To draw a hotspot:

1.   Click the ▣ **Insert Hotspot** button on the **Web Objects** toolbar.

2.   Click and drag to draw a rectangular hotspot region. The Hyperlinks dialog appears.

3.   Click to select the link destination type, and enter the specific hyperlink target (see Selecting a hyperlink target on p. 223).

4.   Click **OK**.

To match a hotspot to an existing shape:

1.   Draw the hotspot as described above, and create the shape as described in Drawing and editing shapes on p. 148.

2.   Select both objects and choose **Fit Hotspot to Shape** from the **Tools** menu.

> The two objects will still be separate, so you can easily delete the shape if it's no longer needed once you've used it as a template to produce a hotspot of a desired shape.

To modify a hotspot hyperlink:

•   Using the Pointer Tool, double-click the hotspot.

The Hyperlinks dialog appears with the current hotspot link target shown.

•   To modify the hyperlink, select a new link destination type and/or target.

•   To remove the hyperlink, change the link destination to **No Hyperlink**.

Editing hotspots

You can move and resize hotspots on the page, just like other objects. A selected hotspot has both an outer bounding box and an inner outline, which serve different purposes.

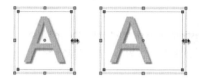

To move or resize a hotspot:

- Click to select the hotspot, then:

    - To move, click and drag from the center, or from the hotspot's bounding box. To constrain the hotspot to vertical or horizontal movement, hold down the **Shift** key while dragging.

    - To resize, click and drag on its outer (bounding box) handles.

By editing the inner outline, you can convert rectangular hotspots into freeform shapes that closely match the parts of the underlying graphic you want to be "hot." To edit the outline, first move the mouse pointer over the hotspot's inner outline until the cursor changes to indicate whether you're over a node or a line.

To create an extra node on a hotspot:

- Click anywhere along the hotspot's outline when you see the cursor.

To change the shape of a hotspot's outline:

- Click and drag a node when you see the ⁻¦⁻ cursor.

Adding rollovers

The term **rollover** refers to an interaction between a mouse and a screen object. For example, you can point your mouse at a graphic on a web page, and see it instantly change color or become a different picture. In more detail, when you point to a web page object, your mouse pointer physically enters the screen region occupied by the object. This triggers an event called a "mouseover" which can trigger some other event—such as swapping another image into the same location. An object whose appearance changes through image-swapping in response to mouse events is called a **rollover graphic**—the **state** of the graphic changes in response to screen events.

You can directly import rollover graphics created in Serif DrawPlus. (See online Help for more information.)

Rollover options

Adding rollovers is basically a matter of deciding which rollover state(s) you'll want to define for a particular object, then specifying an image for each state. WebPlus provides several choices:

Normal State
*is the "resting" state
of the graphic before
any rollover, and is
always defined.*

Over State
*is the state triggered
by a mouseover—
when the mouse
pointer is directly over
the graphic.*

Down State
*is triggered by a
mouse click on the
graphic.*

Another state, **Down+Over** (not illustrated) implies a mouseover that occurs when the graphic is already Down, i.e. after it's been clicked.

You can also specify a **hyperlink** event—for example, a jump to a targeted web page—that will trigger if the user clicks on the object. And you can even group buttons on a page so they work together—and only one button in the group can be 'down' at any one time.

To create a rollover graphic:

1. In a suitable image-editing program, create the variant source images for each state you'll be defining. (See Creating variant graphics on p. 231.)

2. Click **Insert Rollover** on the **Standard Objects** toolbar's Picture flyout.

3. Specify which rollover states (see p. 229) you want to activate for each graphic by checking boxes in the Rollover Graphic dialog. For each one, use the **Browse** button to locate the corresponding source image and specify Export Options for that image (see Setting image export options on p. 177).

4. Check **Embed files in site** if you want to incorporate the image(s) in the site.

5. Check either **Normal** or **Down** as the button's initial rollover state.

6. Click **Set...** to define a hyperlink target for the button.

7. Check **Radio button** if you want to link all the buttons (on a given page) that have this option checked, so that only one of them at a time can be down.

8. Click **OK**. The first time you define a rollover state, you'll see rollover layers established in the document.

WebPlus displays the image assigned to the Normal state. It's a good idea to preview the page and test each rollover object, then return to WebPlus and revise as needed. When you preview or publish the site, WebPlus takes care of exporting one image file for each rollover state, and the HTML file for the published page incorporates the JavaScript code for the rollover event trapping.

To edit a rollover graphic:

1. Right-click (or double-click) the graphic and choose **Edit Rollover...**.

2. Make new selections as needed and click **OK**.

Creating variant source images

For each object with at least one activated rollover state, you'll need to provide a source image. It's the often subtle differences between the Normal image and the "variants" that make the object appear to switch from one state to another. For example, if you've checked the "Over" state for an object, you need to include a variant image that the web page can display when the button is moused over. If you want the button's text to change from black to yellow, then the "Over" state will need an image with yellow text.

Adding popup rollovers

The most common use for popup rollovers in WebPlus is to hover over a picture thumbnail to show its larger representation, usually offset next to the thumbnail. The feature is simple to use and works in a similar way to the more advanced Photo Gallery. Popup rollovers have only two states (normal and hover over) and show the same or a different image made larger in the hover over state; compare this with WebPlus rollovers which have up to four states and only work with identically sized different "variant" images.

WebPlus lets you choose the position and size of the popup in relation to the "hovered over" thumbnail; even the thumbnail can be selected and resized at any time.

With respect to states, WebPlus provides two basic choices:

- **Normal** is the "resting" state of the image before any rollover, and is always defined. A thumbnail can be used but numbered or bullet icons could also be used, perhaps identifying pictures as part of a catalogue, quiz, etc.

- **Over** is the state triggered by a mouseover—when the mouse pointer is directly over the thumbnail the popup "Over" image will appear, disappearing when the mouse pointer moves off the thumbnail.

If captioning is required on popup rollovers this can be made to popup next to your Over image. Caption text can adopt various attributes such as font, bold/italic, size, color.

To create a popup rollover:

1. Click the [icon] **Popup Rollover** button on the **Standard Objects** toolbar's Picture flyout.

2. From the dialog, for the Normal rollover image click the **Browse...** button, and navigate to and select the image. Click **Open...**.

3. For the Over image, the previously chosen Normal image is used by default (typically for photo thumbnails). However, you can **Browse...** to use a completely different image.

4. (Optional) To hyperlink from the Normal image, click the **Set...** button and enter a URL. The user jumps to the hyperlink destination by clicking the image.

5. (Optional) For either image, specify **Export Options...** for that image (see Setting image export options on p. 177).

6. (Optional) Check **Embed image files in site** if you want to incorporate the image(s) in the site.

At this stage you've defined normal and over images to use. However, for popup rollovers to work effectively you'll need to position the Normal and Over images on your page. Positioning is carried out from a dedicated dialog, where each state image can be moved and resized by dragging (or by setting absolute pixel values). Each image adopts a colored border—green for Normal state, blue for Over state.

The dialog additionally shows any previous popup rollovers in its preview window, and offers previously used Left, Top, Width and Height values for easy alignment with the existing popup rollovers.

To position rollover images:

7. In the Rollover Graphic dialog, click the **Set Rollover Position...** button at the bottom of the dialog.

8. From the dialog, select an image. The drop-down list indicates the current selection status, i.e.

    - **Normal Selection**: a Normal image is selected and shows a green border.

    - **Over Selection**: an Over image is selected showing a blue border.

    - **Caption Selection**: caption text is selected showing a red border (only shown with captioning enabled).

    If you deselect an image, the drop-down list shows **No Selection**.

9. Reposition selections by dragging and/or resize selections from corner handles (aspect ratio is always maintained when dragging). Alternatively, enter exact **Left**, **Top**, **Width**, and **Height** values in the input boxes for fine positioning. The box down arrows offer a drop-down list showing the last three values used for Normal, Over, and Captions (from top to bottom)—this lets you align images exactly.

10. (Optional) Check **Position relative to Normal image** to maintain the Over image's position in relation to the Normal image (when the Normal image is resized).

11. (Optional) Uncheck **Maintain aspect ratio** to allow your Normal or Over image resizing to be unconstrained. You have to then use the input boxes (not dragging) to affect unconstrained resizing.

12. Click **OK**. The Normal image will show on your page, but the Over image will only popup after previewing or publishing.

By building up additional Normal images as separate popup rollovers on your web page you can create a stylish popup gallery of images, with each Normal image being part of a sequence of clickable thumbnails.

To edit a popup rollover:

- Double-click the Normal image on the page, to display the Rollover Graphic dialog. Modify settings as appropriate.

To add captioning to Over images:

1. In the Rollover Graphic dialog, check **Display caption with Over image**.

2. Enter your caption text in the **Caption** input box.

3. Set the text attributes for the caption text using the **Font** and **Size** drop-down lists, and the **Bold** and **Italic** check boxes. For applying text color, use the **Text Color** drop-down gallery.

4. Check **Apply Background Color** to enable a color to be selected from the adjacent drop-down gallery.

5. Click **OK**.

The caption text only shows on the Over image, so to position the text on your Over image you'll need to double-click the Normal image on your page. From the dialog, click the **Set Rollover Position...** button and reposition the text (as you would for Normal and Over images). All selected caption text shows with a red border during preview.

12 Adding Dynamic Content

Attaching HTML code

WebPlus lets you attach HTML code to your WebPlus pages, primarily to expand the capabilities of the page, making it more intelligent and interactive. The page can either dynamically generate content or can have its appearance altered within its area as a result of embedded script content.

It's not possible to edit the HTML code itself (there's no real benefit in doing so), but specific areas of the displayed code are editable for additional code to be added, i.e. clearly identifiable placeholders (text surrounded by a white highlight) will show.

In particular, code can be placed at prompted locations in the code such as **_AddCode=** opposite.

The editable areas shown with green text above let you add you own comments or notes.

Any code can be inserted by cut and paste into any of the placeholder positions but typically you can include tokens, HTML code or specific scripts, e.g. JavaScript.

Adding HTML

HTML code for your web page can include fragments either copied from another web page, or perhaps written by yourself. You can also import formatted HTML text from a browser or email program via the Clipboard (for example with a browser's **Select All** and **Copy** commands), using WebPlus's **File>Paste Special...** command.

Before you import your HTML code, WebPlus lets you position an HTML Code Fragment window on your page. Since you won't be able to see the effect of the HTML until you preview the site, be careful to place the window correctly. You'll definitely want to check your web page in a browser! If there's a problem, double-check the code you entered and its position on the WebPlus page (resizing if necessary). If you have some grasp of HTML, examine the page source in a text editor such as Notepad.

To add an HTML code fragment to a page:

1. Copy the HTML code from its original source onto the Clipboard.

2. Click the [<>] **Insert HTML Code** button on the **Web Objects** toolbar.

3. Click on the page or pasteboard to create a new HTML Code Fragment window at a default size or drag to create a sized window.

4. In the dialog, use the **Paste to Head** or **Paste to Body** button to insert the clipboard text into the header of the file or into its body.
   OR
   Use the scrollable code window. Enter one or more HTML code fragments into the appropriate field.

5. Click **OK** to close the dialog. The code will appear on your page in the HTML Code Fragment window.

For more complex scripting, it may be necessary to add supporting files (graphics, text files, etc.) that the inserted script may use—these can be either embedded or linked. This means the files are either kept with the site (embedded) or are referenced externally via a link (much like a hyperlink). Consider your final site size when embedding many images.

To add supporting files:

1. Click the **Add...** button.

2. From the Open dialog, navigate to then select one or more files (use **Ctrl**-click and **Shift**-click for non-contiguous or contiguous selection, respectively). Click **Open**.

3. The files are listed in the **Files** list and will be embedded in your site by default. If you choose not to **Embed** files (making your site smaller), then select each file and click the **Make Linked** button.

4. Click **OK**.

At any point, you can **Add**, **Delete**, and change **Export Options** for any file.

 You can make use of tokens to add a range of variables to your HTML. Use for breadcrumb navigation that will update dynamically if you add, remove or change pages within the site.

Adding JavaScript

To source a vast array of JavaScript code, try searching for "javascript snippets" in your favorite search engine. You should find many thousands of sites hosting freely available code snippets. Most of these sites will clearly indicate what the JavaScript will do for you—they'll also normally let you select the JavaScript code and copy it for pasting directly into the page.

Using IDs

All objects in WebPlus are given unique alphanumeric IDs for referencing by scripting languages. By default, ID generation is automatic for each object, text column, table row and table cell. For example, a newly drawn QuickShape will automatically be assigned an ID of "qs_1", a second QuickShape will be "qs_2", pictures could be "pic_1", "pic_2", etc.

It may be perfectly acceptable to utilize these automatic IDs in your scripts but if you need to assign your own IDs, it's possible to turn off the site-wide automatic generation of IDs in the **HTML Output** tab of the Site Properties dialog (select **Site Properties...** from the **File** menu). Uncheck the option specific for object, text column, table row and/or table cell and press **OK**. Your own replacement IDs can instead be added in the available placeholder, i.e.

```
__AddCode="here"
```

 If the object is copied on the same page or to another website, the ID number will be replaced by a new ID number.

Any object ID can be edited once the object is on the web page. A different name can be used or, if you don't want to show an object's ID (but want to keep site-wide ID generation), you can prevent the ID from being shown in source code.

To edit an object ID:

1. Right-click an object and select **ID...**.

2. In the dialog, modify the HTML ID value.

3. (Optional) Choose whether to **Write ID for this object**. Selecting "Use Site default" means that the setting in the **HTML Output** tab of the Site Properties dialog is honoured—"Yes" or "No" means that the object's ID is always shown or never shown irrespective of the site default setting.

Tokens

WebPlus provides a range of grouped HTML annotation tokens which can be attached to pages. They get replaced by appropriate "real" values when you export to a file or preview your page.

Adding tokens is a simple case of inserting a token string, by copy and paste or typing directly, into one of the placeholder positions in any HTML source.

A full list of such tokens is provided in the WebPlus Help.

Adding forms

Web-based forms allow information to be collected from visitors to your website in an efficient and modern manner. In much the same way as traditional paper forms are used to collect information, Web-based forms offer the same form completion concepts, but take advantage of the Internet as a powerful information conduit. Some common form types include request forms, feedback forms, and guest books.

Form data can be collected in a variety of ways—by email, to a local/remote script file, or via Serif Web Resources.

Form Structure

The building blocks of a form comprise a mixture of text, graphics and form controls. Form controls are intelligent as they collect web visitor data and can be added, moved and modified in a similar way to familiar objects in WebPlus such as graphics and table elements. A control can be a button, edit box, text area, combo box, check box, radio button, CAPTCHA object, or File browser. A typical form, perhaps a email feedback form, is made up of a combination of some of these controls.

Email form

Name

Email Address

Comments

Submit   Reset

From the web visitor's perspective, information is typed into text boxes or selected from check boxes, radio buttons, or drop-down boxes. The information entered can be numeric, textual, or a mixture of both, depending on the type of field. The tab order by which fields are to be completed is configurable, as is validation of input data (see WebPlus help for more about tab order and validation).

Each field has its own set of properties relating to its appearance, its value(s), validation, or the action expected of the field.

A form's functionality only becomes active when your website is published (of course you can still preview your forms from within WebPlus, see Previewing your site on p. 289). When a web visitor enters data into, or selects a form option, the data will be sent back to a chosen destination when the form is submitted.

JavaScript can be used to allow interactivity in your web forms. It drives formatting, validation, calculations, and actions—all key functions in Web-based form development.

Where is data sent?

After submission, form data can be sent to one of the following:

- an email address (of the web developer).

- a script file (stored locally or remotely); this could write text to a text file or into a server database.

- Serif Web Resources; for transit of form data to your email (via Serif).

As is standard in web form management, it is possible to set the encoding type, target window/frames, submission methods (POST or GET) can be used.

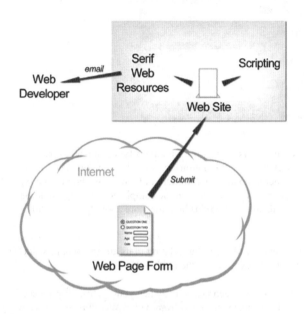

Creating forms

Several methods exist for creating forms: you can create a pre-defined ready-to-go **standard** form (opposite), select individual form controls for your form, or create a form from scratch; the first two methods use an easy-to-use Form Wizard.

Standard forms are available for Contact information, User comments, CV submission, Opinion, and Address forms.

To create a standard form:

1. Click the  **Form Wizard** on the **Web Objects** toolbar's Form flyout.

2. In the dialog, click the **Use and adapt a standard form** icon and then **Next>**.

3. From the list of forms, select a form type while using the lower Preview pane.

```
Comments 1
Comments 2
Contact 1
Contact 1b
Credit Card
CV Submission 1
CV Submission 2
Opinion 1
UK Contact Form 1
UK Contact Form 2
UK Contact Form 3
```

4. Click **Next>**.

5. In the next screen, choose to add, modify or delete controls.

   - To add, click a button in the **Add** box.

   - To modify a standard object, select an existing control in the window and choose **Edit Control...**. See Editing form controls on p. 248 for more information.

   - To delete a standard object, select an existing control in the window and choose **Delete** (or press the **Delete** key).

   - To rearrange the control order, use the **Move Up** and **Move Down** buttons.

6. After clicking **Next>**, choose a destination for your form data by clicking a destination button. Select **Finish** to complete the wizard.

7. To insert the form at a default size, position the form place cursor and click the mouse.

If you're looking for design freedom, WebPlus provides a blank form and form objects from which you can design your form from scratch. You can add form controls or standard form objects, or both. See WebPlus help for more details.

To create a custom form (via Form Wizard):

1. Click the **Form Wizard** on the **Web Objects** toolbar's Form flyout.

2. In the dialog, click the **Create a new form with the wizard** icon and then **Next>**.

3. In the next screen, you need to add form controls that will make up your form. In the Add box, either:

   • For a ready-to-go form control, click the **Pre-defined** button, and pick your chosen form control. You'll need to double-click the new control in the window to name the control.
   OR

   • Click on one of the other form controls to create from scratch. See Form controls on p. 245 for a description of each control.

4. In the dialog, use the internal name for the control (to uniquely identify it), or edit it and enter a label to accompany the control (this is shown on-screen). You can also edit the control by using the **Edit Control** button. Editing a control allows validation, control of form length, and other control attributes to be set. See Editing form controls on p. 248 for more information. If you've edited a value, click **OK**.

5. Repeat the above for each chosen form control as needed. They will be listed (in order of creation) in the upper window.
   Before continuing, you have to add a Submit form control to your form. This is vital to pass data to its destination. Click the **Submit Button** to automatically add the button to your form. It is normal practice to accompany this with a **Reset Button**, used to clear out form fields of data not yet submitted. Click **Next>**.

6. From the next dialog, choose a destination for your form data by clicking a destination button for email, script file (local or remote) or Serif Web Resources and a name to define the whole form. (See Submission of forms on p. 248).

7. Select **Finish** to complete the wizard.

8. To insert the form at a default size, position the form place cursor where you want the form to appear on the page, then simply click the mouse.

Form controls

Each form control is an "intelligent" object which differs from other WebPlus objects. They are intelligent because they can store visitor input and pass it on to a central location during form submission. Controls can be moved as for other objects but cannot have colors or transparency applied, borders adjusted, or resized.

A range of form controls are available from within the Form Wizard or directly from the **Web Objects** toolbar's Form flyout. You assign an internal unique name to each field and then set a variety of properties—each form control has its own set which can be modified.

Form Control Icon	Form Control Name	When to use?
	Form Button	Use when specifying an action that can be triggered by a button click. A whole range of buttons of varying design and function can be created.
		Submit and Reset buttons are available in the Form wizard. They perform form submission and clear all form data, respectively.
	Edit Box	Use for entering single-line text, numbers, or a mixture of both. Someone's surname would be a good example.

	Text Area	Use for adding multi-line text, numbers or a mixture of both. Generally used for entering input, either textual or numerical, e.g. an enquiry, recipe, or list of figures.
	Combo Box	For selection from a list of items in a drop-down menu where only one item can be selected by default, e.g. a gender combo.

Combo boxes also allow for a scrollable list of items; with optional support for multiple selection. For example, to select Afghanistan, Algeria, and Andorra, use **Ctrl**-click on each item:

You can use **Shift**-click to group select a range of items.

> When designing multiple selection combo boxes, drag the top or bottom of the Combo box to allow several items to be displayed by default.

	Check Box	Ideal when you want to select multiple items displayed side by side. A good alternative to a Combo Box if space allows. The web visitor clicks once to select or deselect the box, e.g.

☑ *Would you like to be notified of any upcoming events in the near future?*

Radio Button

Good for selection of a single mutually exclusive item from a grouped subset of choices. For example, a set of radio buttons can be used to obtain gender information from the web visitor.

Male
Female

 File Browser

Use the File browser to have your web visitors upload any file from their computers. The visitor simply navigates via a **Browse...** button and selects a local file of their choice. Some examples include uploading pictures, CVs, drawings and instructions.

CAPTCHA

Use as a security check for protecting against spamming. The form control offers a random text string for the web visitor to reproduce in a text box. Passing the check initiates form submission, which can only be via Serif Web Resources form submission.

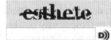

 Alternatively, enable the security check during form submission instead (see Submission of forms on p. 248). Only use one method when using forms.

Hidden objects can be added as a form control if you use the Form Wizard. Although the web visitor does not see the field, it is typically used by the web developer to ensure the data collected has an identifiable string stored with the visitor's data. An example could be a publish date relating to the web page—useful for identifying incorrectly working pages.

In addition, hidden fields can be added by right-clicking on the entire form and selecting **Edit Form Properties....** The dialog's **Hidden Fields** tab allows for input of any number of hidden fields.

Editing form controls

Each form control type (buttons, text field, etc.) has different characteristics and therefore different values for editing. Values can be changed as you create the form or at a later time after the control has been added to the form.

The Form Wizard's **Edit Control...** button lets you modify the control during form creation. Alternatively, the control can be edited later by right-clicking on the form control on the web page and choosing the Edit option, e.g. Edit Text Box.

Submission of forms

All forms have one thing in common—they must be submitted to allow data to be collected. To do this you can either create a **Submit Button** unaided or more usually use the ready-made button in the Form Wizard. The button needs to be present on the form and is typically used with a Reset button to clear all form controls of data.

Form data submission is possible via several methods.

No action

Form data is not submitted. This option is useful if you want to temporarily disable data collection or if you haven't yet set up scripting or Serif Web Resources. At a later time you can edit the form (right-click then choose **Edit Form Properties...**) and select a valid submission method.

email address

Use this option to bypass the usual POST/GET submission methods. When the Submit button is pressed the web visitor's default email program is launched. The form data (passed in a single string) is added to the email body and is ready to be sent to the configured email destination. Especially useful if there is no local or remote scripting in place.

 This is an unsecure submission method—any private or confidential information will be not be encrypted.

To set up email directly:

1. With the icon enabled, add a **Form name**.

2. Enter the destination **Email address** (or select an already known email address from the drop-down menu).

Serif Web Resources

Not everyone will have access to or even want to operate their own web server so, as an alternative to this, you can use Serif Web Resources. This is a free web to email gateway service which will transit valued form data via Serif and send it to your personal email address(es)—the service does require that you firstly have a Serif Web resources login (for security reasons), which will allow you to create, edit and delete your own email destinations; these are called Form Email Targets.

To set up Serif Web Resources:

1. With the **Serif Web Resources** icon enabled, add a **Form name**.

2. Click the **Select** button (log in to Serif Web Resources if you're not already logged in).

3. From the dialog, enter your target address details:

    • Enter a target email address in the **Email Address** box.

    • Enter a **Custom subject**, the subject line string that you'll see in your web visitor's email, e.g. Email Submission from Rainbow_WWW: Contact Details.

    • Add a **Confirmation message** which will be displayed to the web visitor after they click their Submit button.

    • In the **Language** field set the language in which the confirmation message will be sent.

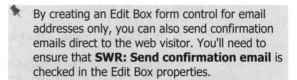 By creating an Edit Box form control for email addresses only, you can also send confirmation emails direct to the web visitor. You'll need to ensure that **SWR: Send confirmation email** is checked in the Edit Box properties.

Check **Reply to me** in the above dialog to make the Reply-to field of the confirmation email set to the web developer's email. This allows the visitor to contact the web developer directly via email.

4. Click **Add new**. The email entry is created and added to the Available Email Targets list. You'll notice that the entry is classed as "*Not Confirmed*". Before the service commences, you'll get a email confirmation message sent to your email address. By clicking the link, the service will be activated and the entry will change to "*Confirmed.*"

5. (Optional) Repeat the above procedure to add further email targets, then select an email entry to make it active.

6. Click **OK** to exit.

To enable CAPTCHA security on submission:

1. Check **Use CAPTCHA Gateway** to enable a security check as the web visitor submits the form. This protects against spamming. A dialog offers a random text string for the web visitor to reproduce in an text box. Passing the check initiates form submission.

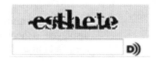

2. Choose a submission method, encoding type, and target window/frame.

Incidentally, the web visitor will receive a basic confirmation page generated by Serif Web Resources to acknowledge successful receipt of form data. As a useful tip you can create and assign your very own acknowledgment web page to be used instead of this basic page. Your own page is just like any other web page so you can add your own information, and design the page in the same style and appearance as the rest of your site.

To add your own acknowledgement page:

1. Right-click on the form (must submit data via Serif Web Resources) and choose **Edit Form Properties...**.

2. Switch to the Hidden Fields tab, click the **Add...** button and add the word "redirect" to the **Name** field and your intended target URL with http:// prefix (i.e., the web address of your own acknowledgement page) in the **Value** field.

3. Click **OK**. The new web page will display on the next form submission.

★ No personal data will be stored on Serif web servers. All form data is redirected in real time.

Script file from my hard drive

This option is for experienced web developers with scripting expertise.

To set up a local script file:

1. With the **Script file** icon enabled, add a Form name.

2. Navigate to your local script file, typically a .cgi, .pl, .dll, or .exe file with the **Browse...** button.

3. Check **Embed** to include the script within the site. If unchecked, the script file will be unconnected to the site (any updates to the script will be invisible to the site).

4. Optionally, the **Export Options...** button lets you define a web file name and folder for the script.

5. Choose a submission method, encoding type, target window/frame, and Character set.

A Remote script

Use if your ISP will not allow you to run your own scripts on your ISP web space. Instead, your ISP may supply a basic script file that can be linked to from your web page. Typically, the script will send the form data back to your email address (already setup with your ISP).

To set up a remote script file:

1. With the **Remote script** icon enabled, add a Form name.

2. Enter a URL pointing directly to a script file, typically a .cgi, .pl, .dll, or .exe file.

3. Choose a submission method, encoding type, target window/frame, and Character set.

RSS feeds and podcasts

Really Simple Syndication (RSS) feeds are streams of constantly changing news and information which are very popular on fast-paced websites. The popularity of RSS feeds is evident if you use Internet-based news services regularly. You'll see RSS feeds indicated on websites by a ⬛ symbol—by clicking the symbol the user may be able to manually or automatically subscribe to that RSS feed via a RSS Reader.

Podcasts are syndication feeds just like RSS feeds but offer slightly different options that reflect a podcast's use of digital media such as audio and video files. Put simply, RSS feeds will publish articles, while podcasts will broadcast information as episodes.

In WebPlus, you can create your own RSS feeds or podcasts that you can frequently publish and update. In essence, you become the publisher (rather than the reader) of one or more information services containing headlines, site summaries or your very own articles. For podcasts, you broadcast media clips as episodes.

The example shows a constantly updating fictitious school's podcast with clickable links to media (both audio and video).

RSS feeds and podcasts can be configured in a very similar way in WebPlus. In fact, the process for creating your own RSS feed or podcast utilizes the same **RSS Feed Tool** within WebPlus.

If you want to reuse a third party RSS feeds/podcasts and add it to your own web page, a reader can be embedded into your web page by using the **RSS Reader Tool**.

Bluewood School Podcast

WW2 soldier Interview (audio)

22 September 2009, 10:59:53 | history_group@bluewood.sch.uk ➔

Our history group got the chance to spend some time with Arthur Peel, a WWII veteran, having served with 7th Armoured Division (aka the Desert Rats) in North Africa against Field Marshall Rommel.

🎧 Interview_soldier.mp3 (Pending)

SpaceZone Trip

11 September 2009, 10:51:37 | cassy@bluewood.sch.uk ➔

Bluewood takes to the stars in a one-day visit to the SpaceZone. Find out how Year 10 built their own rocket.

🎧 Space.mp3 (Pending)

Yorkminster trip (video)

09 September 2009, 10:46:24 | cassy@bluewood.sch.uk ➔

Year 10's trip to York to learn about the history of Yorkminster.

📎 Yorkminster.mp4 (Pending)

Major's Visit (video)

07 September 2009, 10:44:14 | Paul.Chalmers@bluewood.sch.uk ➔

Find out how Bluewood welcomed the Major to the school. A big focus was put on the current school - community projects.

📎 Major_visit.mp4 (Pending)

Browser support for feeds

As an emergent technology, feeds will only be viewable in the latest versions of Internet browsers. Here is a simple list outlining browsers and their versions which can read a feed within its own browser (with no third-party plug-ins required).

- Internet Explorer 7.0 (or later)

- Mozilla Firefox (all versions)

- Opera 8.0 (or later)

If you are using a previous version of the above don't worry! There are a range of feed readers available via the Internet (type "RSS reader" into your favorite search engine) which will work equally well.

Creating RSS feeds or podcasts

The **RSS Feed Tool** enables you to create one or more RSS feeds/podcasts from which web visitors can subscribe via their standalone feed reader, web browsers or Apple iTunes® 7 or above. As you create a feed a series of settings can be applied to the feed which relate to feed title/descriptions, associated images, copyright information, categories, keywords, etc.

To insert an RSS feed or podcast:

1. Click the 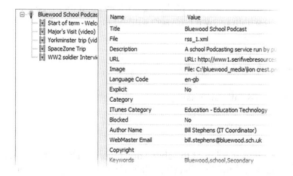 **RSS Feed Tool** button on the **Web Objects** toolbar's RSS flyout.

2. Click the **Add RSS Feed** or **Add Podcast** button to create a new RSS feed or podcast entry. A new feed name called **New RSS Feed** or **New Podcast** appears in the left-hand menu. With the entry selected, you'll see a list of settings for the new entry which can be modified by clicking in the Value column. Drop-down lists, dialog boxes or text input boxes let you add, select or modify values for the feed.

    For example, a podcast feed and listed episodes for a school's podcasting service would look as follows:

Name	Value
Title	Bluewood School Podcast
File	rss_1.xml
Description	A school Podcasting service run by p
URL	URL: http://www1.serifwebresource
Image	File: C:\bluewood_media\lion crest.p
Language Code	en-gb
Explicit	No
Category	
ITunes Category	Education - Education Technology
Blocked	No
Author Name	Bill Stephens (IT Coordinator)
WebMaster Email	bill.stephens@bluewood.sch.uk
Copyright	
Keywords	Bluewood,school,Secondary

Left-hand tree:
- Bluewood School Podcast
  - Start of term - Welc
  - Major's Visit (video)
  - Yorkminster trip (vid
  - SpaceZone Trip
  - WW2 soldier Intervi

You'll notice a series of episodes listed under the podcast feed (Bluewood School Podcast). We'll look at how to add these later.

3. Click **OK**.

4. To place the feed on the page, position the ⬛ cursor and simply click the mouse. A ⬊ or 🍦 button appears at the cursor position (for an RSS feed or podcast, respectively).

💡 For one-click automatic subscription of podcasts, label your podcast symbol indicating which application the subscription will be made to.

To swap the feed for another:

*   Once an RSS feed or podcast exists, double-click the feed on the page to redirect the button to another feed. Simply select a different entry and click **OK**.

    For podcasts, the dialog can also automatically subscribe the podcast to the visitor's Google Reader, My Yahoo!, or iTunes application. Pick from the **Open Podcast with** drop-down list. Otherwise, for manual subscription of RSS feeds or podcasts, the RSS Standard option is used.

Once the RSS feed or podcast is created, articles or episodes (respectively) can be added to the feed and then published. Once updated, you'll need to republish your web page (see Publishing to the web on p. 291).

To add or update articles or episodes:

1. Click the ⬊ **RSS Feed Tool** button on the WebPlus's **Web Objects** toolbar.

2. From the RSS Feed dialog, ensure the correct feed is selected, then click the **RSS Feed Manager** button.

3. At the right of the dialog, click the **Add Article** or **Add Episode** button. This creates a new entry, provisionally titled New Article (for an RSS feed) or New Episode (for podcast) under the selected feed.

4. Edit your article/episode and its settings (see above). Drop-down lists, dialog boxes or text input boxes let you add, select or modify values for the feed.

Again, using the above school podcast example, the associated first episode could have been added with the following settings.

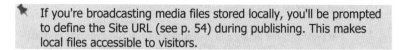

Name	Value
Item Title	Yorkminster trip (video)
Description	Year 10's trip to York to learn about the
Media file	File: C:\bluewood_media\2009\Yorkmins
Duration	00:22:12
Publication Date	09/09/2009 10:46:24
Explicit	No
Category	school trips
Blocked	No
Author E-mail	cassy@bluewood.sch.uk
Author Name	Cassy McDonald (Y10 head teacher)
Keywords	Yorkminster, cathedrals, history, religion
Summary	The trip was arranged so pupils can und

5. Click **OK**, then click **OK** again.

> ★ If you're broadcasting media files stored locally, you'll be prompted to define the Site URL (see p. 54) during publishing. This makes local files accessible to visitors.

Submission of podcast feeds

For podcasts via iTunes, as a broadcaster you'll need to have your podcast submitted to iTunes. The podcast feed has to be reviewed by iTunes staff to check for technical problems, an acceptable login, inappropriate use of explicit language, offensive material, and misuse of copyright material. This step means that if your feed is approved, iTunes users will then be able to subscribe to your podcast feed.

To submit a podcast feed to iTunes:

1. Launch iTunes.

2. Click on **Podcasts** in the LIBRARY section.

3. Select the **Podcast Directory** button at the bottom of the iTunes workspace.

4. Scroll down to the bottom of the window and in the FOR PODCASTERS box, click **Submit a Podcast**.

5. In the next screen, paste your Feed URL into the **Podcast Feed URL** box. Your Feed URL will be a URL with an xml file name (e.g., rss_1.xml) at its end.

6. Click **Continue**.

Subscribing

Subscribing to RSS feeds and Podcasts

Web visitors can subscribe to these feeds by a variety of methods.

Subscription type	Method
manual	The visitor simply clicks on a diagnostic symbol which indicates the type of feed, i.e.
	For RSS Feeds
	For podcasts
	Your published RSS feed or podcast offers a clickable subscription button, e.g.
	Subscribe to this feed
	This lets you add the feed to your browser's favorites.
automatic (podcasts only)	An icon (or associated hyperlink) is clicked according to the visitor's preferred chosen subscription. The podcast and reader is defined explicitly, so subscription is automatic. An example could be as follows:

Google Reader
(One-click subscription)

My Yahoo!
(One-click subscription)

ITunes
(One-click subscription)

Instead of a direct button, a hyperlink (see p. 223) can be created from anywhere in your site which links directly to your new feed. A special link destination type called **RSS Feed** is used.

Subscribing via iTunes

Once a broadcaster has submitted their feed to iTunes and had it approved, the web visitor can subscribe to the podcast as follows:

1. Launch iTunes.

2. Click **Subscribe to Podcast...** from the **Advanced** menu.

3. Enter the feed URL in the dialog's input box, then click **OK**. The podcast appears as an entry in the window.

New episodes can be downloaded via GET or GET ALL buttons next to each episode or feed, respectively (you can also right-click on a feed and choose Update Podcast. Media files will then be downloaded and will be available for playback directly within iTunes.

To unsubscribe to the feed, use the **Unsubscribe** button at the bottom of the window.

Including third-party feeds

Instead of creating your own RSS feed or podcast you may wish to include an RSS feed from another website on your own web page—a web page's content can be boosted by inclusion of a feed from any popular news service (Reuters, BBC News, sport, etc.) or other information service (e.g., financial). Many major news and information services host lists of RSS feeds relating to specific areas of interest (geographical, entertainment, political, music, etc.) so it's just a case of copying the link for the website's RSS feed and pasting it into a dialog shown when clicking the WebPlus's **RSS Reader Tool**. Please bear in mind any terms and conditions in using a third-party RSS feed—these should be clearly indicated on the originating website.

The addition of the RSS feed reader to your page automatically subscribes yourself to the chosen RSS feed or podcast. There are other ways of subscribing to RSS feeds or podcasts via web browsers and iTunes, but here we'll focus on how to include the feed on your page and have it automatically receive articles or episodes.

Here's an example of a financial RSS feed added to a WebPlus web page:

To include an RSS feed or podcast on your page:

1. Locate an RSS feed available on web pages of popular news and information services. Look for one of the following distinctive buttons, e.g.

2. Copy and paste the Feed URL from a web page to the clipboard. For Internet Explorer, you can right-click on a subscribe button/link and choose **Copy Shortcut**. For Mozilla Firefox, choose **Copy Link Location** via right-click.

3. Click the **RSS Reader Tool** button on the **Web Objects** toolbar's RSS flyout.

4. In the dialog, paste the Feed URL into the **RSS Feed URL** field.

5. (Optional) Select a different color, font, font size, or font style for the feed's Title, Headline, or Summary Color.

6. (Optional) Set the local time zone for your site in the **Time Zone** drop-down list.

7. (Optional) Change the **Date Format** (MM/DD or DD/MM) for the article's published date that shows in the article's header.

8. Click **OK**.

9. A ⟨⟨⟩⟩ cursor is displayed. To insert the feed in a window of default size, simply click the mouse.
   OR
   More typically, to set the size of the feed window, drag out a region and release the mouse button.

The feed window will be filled with a peach color with the URL shown—you'll need to publish the page to view the current new feed. Remember that the content will update automatically as the feed is updated on the original website. A typical published podcast feed could look as follows (but will update frequently):

When the web visitor views the feed each episode can be played by clicking on the audio link, typically pointing to an MP3 file. Once downloaded and saved, the file can be played on a currently set default player (e.g., Windows Media Player).

Understanding e-commerce

E-commerce entails the buying and selling of goods on the Internet. It's difficult to escape online retailing in any Internet session these days—you've more than likely used some form of Internet shopping at some point, when buying online CDs, books, holidays, etc. Any site that supports this kind of e-commerce activity will typically make use of a shopping cart system and a payment processing system. A shopping cart is a virtual basket (think of a supermarket basket) which stores your chosen items and is used in conjunction with a payment processing system (taking the place of the supermarket's checkout).

For major companies, the shopping cart technology is developed in-house (maybe the payment processing is carried out by a third party company). For smaller companies or organizations, the shopping cart is normally a brought-in third-party solution due to the cost/resource limitations. There are many third-party shopping cart providers that can be used—all account-based and equipped to accept credit cards instead of using a traditional payment gateway (e.g., by phone).

So where does WebPlus fit into all this? Firstly, WebPlus allows you to choose one of several specially chosen shopping cart providers and, secondly, it allows you to connect to the shopping cart provider via a form or link on the WebPlus page. Forms allow for buying options (colors, quantity) to be set, as well as calculate tax rates, shipping, bulk items, etc. Links offer simple one-click purchasing without buying options. The features are provider-specific and as a result vary widely.

Configuring your shopping cart provider

A number of different shopping cart providers can be configured within WebPlus. These are the most commonly used and some, like PayPal®, you may have come across directly as an eBay® customer. The configuration process directs you to the provider's own site from where you can sign-up as a registered user.

 Use the provider's website to find out more about unique shopping cart features.

To setup a shopping cart provider:

1. Click the **Configure E-Commerce** button on the **Web Objects** toolbar's E-Commerce flyout.

2. From the **E-Commerce Configuration** dialog, you have two options depending on whether you are an existing or new user of one of the shopping cart providers, i.e.

    •   If you're a new user, choose a shopping cart provider by enabling its radio button, then click the **Sign Up Now** button. The provider's web site is shown in a new browser window from where you can register with the shopping cart provider.

    •   If you're an existing user, enable the button next to your chosen provider, and click **Next>**. This option simply sets the default provider for your site (rather than set up a provider account).

3. The subsequent dialog is provider-specific and may show offline testing options, window selection, store IDs, currency options and/or tax choices.

4. Click the **Finish** button to complete shopping cart configuration.

As an example, choosing PayPal lets you define an email address to receive payments, or use a "Sandbox", a test tool, for trying out your shopping cart before going live (otherwise you may start making money before you're ready!). Click the **Find Out More** button to setup a separate Sandbox login in addition to your "live" PayPal login.

Once you've configured the shopping cart, you'll need to Insert an e-commerce form.

Inserting an e-commerce object (PayPal)

The creation of e-commerce objects within WebPlus takes a Wizard-based approach. An e-commerce object can be added to the web page as a form or link (i.e., a simple button or any object's hyperlink) by completion of a series of dialogs. Whether you choose to use forms or links depends on the characteristics of the items you are planning to sell, and how you want to sell your goods.

For example, if you are a trader wishing to sell a quantity of bricks you could create an **E-Commerce button** (as a Buy Now link). This option would make an assumption about the potential transaction, i.e. that all the bricks

are the same style/color and that the buyer would wish to purchase a fixed amount.

This is because a link is only a button and cannot host any "interactive" buying options that would be need for more complex purchases. One buyer's click will buy a standard product offering—nothing more. Useful in some situations but in others completely inadequate.

More complex purchases using **E-Commerce Forms** offer user interactivity coupled with flexibility. If we take the brick trader as an example again, a form can be used to host quantity and brick style/color options so that the customer has control and can get what he/she wants!

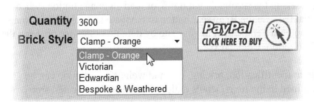

Here the web visitor has chosen to buy 3600 bricks of style "Clamp - Orange."

The dialog that is displayed when you add an e-commerce object will entirely depend on the currently enabled shopping cart provider (see Configuring your Shopping Cart provider on p. 261).

 The following procedures assume that PayPal is configured as your shopping cart.

To insert an e-commerce object:

1. Click the **Insert an E-Commerce object** button on the **Web Objects** toolbar's E-Commerce flyout.

2. In the **Add PayPal Object** dialog, pick the email address which is to receive the payment information. WebPlus will already assume that the email address set during shopping cart configuration is used. Alternatively, uncheck the **Use the site default account** box and set a different email address to override the site default.

3. Pick an object type from the PayPal Form box. Select a "Form" radio button if you want to create an **E-Commerce Form** which will contain buying options (e.g., color or quantity). If the product for sale has no buying options then you can use a "Link" object (i.e., to create a clickable **E-Commerce Button**).

4. (Optional). If a Form or Button is not what you are looking for, enable the last option instead to paste code in a subsequent dialog. This would be code generated from PayPal's website (look under Merchant Tools). Click **Next>**.

5. In the next dialog, define a button for use. It's possible to enable a standard text button (when enabled, enter any text string), a standard image button (when enabled, pick from an attractive selection of presets in the scrollable window), or load an image button (when enabled, use the **Browse...** button to navigate and select your image). Images are embedded in your site by default; otherwise uncheck the last option. Click **Next>**.

6. Item identification, pricing, tax, and weight information can be defined in the Item Details dialog. Options to be selected are:

   • **Item Name**: The item name for sale. Shown on the form and shopping cart.

   • **Allow customer to specify the item name**: Check to swap the above Item Name for a box in which the web visitor can enter their own item name (also good for specifying donation details).

   • **Item ID**: Add an easily identifiable string to track the item through PayPal.

- **Currency**: Set the currency in which the transaction will be made in.

- **Price**: The price for the item. Shown on-screen by default.

- **Allow customer to specify the amount**: Check to swap the above Price for a box in which the web visitor can enter their own price. Use with donation forms, where the customer sets the amount.

- **Override the tax settings..**: Check to override provider's profile's tax setting for the item. If checked, specify a flat tax rate for the item, e.g. 0% for tax-free charitable donations.

- **Weight**: Set an item weight if you're using weight-based shipping (US only), set in your PayPal profile. Typically, pounds (lb) are used as measurement, but kilograms (kg) can also be set if needed.

Choose from the above settings and click **Next>**.

7. For e-commerce forms only, two subsequent dialogs are shown:

- The Item Description dialog lets you optionally include an image (e.g., to preview the item for sale), and short and long descriptions that will show in the form. Click **Next>**.

- The Item Options dialog lets you create edit boxes, combo boxes, radio buttons, and fixed names (up to 10 options can be selected per form in PayPal; only one price-changing option) as appropriate—you can design from scratch or use previously saved options fields. Click **Next>**.

8. In the Item Details dialog, set a default quantity in the input box, or check the box to let the user specify an amount at checkout.
OR
Set the Add Edit box option to let the customer define the quantity to be ordered.

For shipping and handling associated with the order, enter a set amount for Handling, Shipping, and Extra Shipping charges.
If left blank, the default PayPal's profile will be used instead. Click **Next>**.

9. In the Extra Customer Information dialog, choose to prompt the customer for an address, don't prompt, or require the customer to enter an address. Optionally, ask a question of the customer in the text box. Click **Next>**.

10. The Payment Pages dialog offers some payment settings, i.e.

    • Enter the name of your Checkout Page Style (if setup in advance via your PayPal login).

    • Set a language for the PayPal login page. Pick for the drop-down list.

    • Change the text for the Continue button on the Successful Payment Page.

    • If needed, define Successful Payment Pages and/or Cancelled Payment Pages. Enter the page's URL or select an entry from the drop-down list.

12. For e-commerce forms only, choose a form layout from the Form Layout dialog. Several check box options let you control what gets shown on the form layout, e.g you can disable the item's price.

13. Click **Finish**.

14. To insert the form or button, position the cursor where you want it to appear on the page, then simply click the mouse.

To edit an e-commerce form or button:

1. Select the form, right-click the form and choose **Edit E-Commerce Form...**.
   OR
   Select the button, right-click the button and choose **Edit E-Commerce Button...**.

2. Modify e-commerce settings screen-by-screen in the displayed dialog.

To convert to a standard form:

- Right-click on the existing e-commerce form and choose **Convert to Form**.

Using Smart objects

For modern interactive web features (counters, forums, blogs, and more), WebPlus uses server-sided **Smart objects** placed on the page. Smart objects store gathered web visitor data on Serif's own secure server space. These objects are available from **Serif Web Resources**, a secure online service for not just creating and inserting smart objects, but for storing and managing object data once your site is published and live.

Let's look at each Smart object you'll find in Web Resources and what you can do with them.

Name	Use
Active Viewers	Use to show how many people are currently viewing the web page.
Blog	A blog acts as a personal journal on your web page which hosts your own published articles in an easy-to-use RTF editor. Articles can be commented on by visitors to the web page. With blogs you can: - Add your own personal **profile**. - Add **social bookmarking links**. - Use article **trackbacks** for inter-blog cross-referencing; use receive trackbacks. - Use **tagging** to categorize articles for easier user access. - Enable users to subscribe to articles (most recent articles/comments) via RSS feed readers.

- Enable CAPTCHA anti-spam protection.

- Apply a **Visual Styles** (theme) to your blog.

- Use **Editor groups** for multi-author article publishing (see p. 285).

Forum*

Add a thread-based discussion forum to your site, optionally in a full-sized window. With forums you can:

- Under different **categories** (e.g., Motoring) add multiple **subforums** (Classics, Convertibles, Custom, etc.).

- Establish **access control** for users and moderators (see p. 285).

- Set forum **privacy** as publicly readable or private.

- Apply a **theme** (style) to the overall forum object.

- Create, edit, and assign **user ranks**.

- Set **user permissions**.

Users can view number of topics, posts, and last post submitted, and obviously post to the forum.

Hit Counter

A straightforward count of the number of hits on the current page (reset as needed). Different styles can be adopted.

News

Add a news window onto your page. The object supports RTF editing as well as paragraph styles, hyperlinks, inserted media, and even HTML source editing.

Poll

Set up an online poll to canvass web visitor's opinions.

Shout Box

Acts as an interactive chat window similar to Windows Messenger. Let your web visitors chat amongst themselves.

User List

The User List Smart object operates in two modes (each mode selectable via a pop-up dialog):

- **Mailing List mode**: Have website visitors sign up to newsletters, party confirmations, information request, and many more. Lists can be controlled manually or by self-subscription.

- **Access Control mode**: Control accessibility to pages, forums, and blogs by using user groups. See Access Control on p. 276 for more details.

  - Enable CAPTCHA anti-spam protection during user registration.

  - Create user groups (with optional user sign-up, auto-login, and connection to Smart objects).

  - Add, remove, suspend, or ban users.

For security reasons, the objects are only available via a **Serif Web Resources** login accessible from within WebPlus. If you don't have a valid username and password you must create a Web Resources account first.

- If your email address is already known to Serif (maybe you've just registered or have registered previously) you'll be asked for a limited number of questions to complete account registration.

- If you're new to Serif and unregistered you'll have to complete full security as required. Full instructions are provided on login screens.

To create a Serif Web Resources account:

1. Click ![Smart Object Tool icon] **Smart Object Tool** on the **Web Objects** toolbar.

2. In the login dialog, click the **Create Account** link under the login boxes.

3. In the next dialog, enter your current email address and a password twice. You'll need to review and agree to Serif's terms and conditions of use (via a check box).

4. Click the **Signup** button.

5. An additional dialog, will ask for personal details, plus a few check boxes if you would like to receive the Serif Community newsletter, Serif offers, and/or other third-party offers.

6. A confirmation email will be sent to your email address. Click the link in the email and you're ready to login to Serif Web Resources (by clicking the Smart Object Tool again).

To clear Account details:

- Go to **Tools>Options** and click **Clear Account Details** shown from the **Options>General** menu option. This will clear the stored login details for Serif Web Resources so that automatic login will no longer work. Details will need to be entered next time so be sure you've remembered your password.

To access Web Resources:

1. Click ![Smart Object Tool icon] **Smart Object Tool** on the **Web Objects** toolbar.

2. At the login prompt enter your username and your password. Check **Remember account details** to access Web Resources directly in future (bypassing the login screen).

3. Click the **Login** button. The Smart Objects dialog is displayed.

Once created, you can check your account details from the Smart Objects dialog by clicking the **My Account** button.

Creating Smart objects

Think of a Smart object as being a general term for elements that you'll use on your page—as discussed previously. Smart objects are not added directly to the page from Serif Web Resources, but are first added to your own object library (the library lets you manage and edit each object)—objects can then be added to the web page immediately or at a later date.

 Some Smart objects are conditional on another Smart object being created first. An example is the Forum Smart Object which requires the User List smart object to be created first.

Smart objects can be organized into categorized **profiles**. These are useful if you're managing multiple websites, where smart objects can be grouped together under a profile per site.

To create Smart object profiles:

1. From the main Smart Objects dialog, click the **Manage Profiles** button at the bottom of the My Smart Objects Library pane.

2. Click **New profile**, then enter a new **Name** in the text box.

3. Click **Save**, then click **Exit**.

The profile is added to the top of the My Smart Object Library pane. You can then add existing Smart objects into your new profile by drag and drop.

To add an object to the library:

1. From the main Smart Objects dialog, click the **New...** button.

2. In the **Create Smart Object** dialog, use the scroll bar to navigate the list, then select a Smart object.

3. (Optional) For your Smart object to operate in a language other than English, select from the **Language** drop-down menu.

4. Select **OK**. Depending on the type of object selected, a different Create dialog will be displayed showing options specific to the Smart object.

5. From the dialog:

- Enter your own **Name** for the object.

- (Optional) Select a **Profile** from the drop-down menu if created previously.

- (Optional) A **Filter Offsite** string (access to the object will be restricted to the domain entered and will prevent the URL from being copied).

- (Optional) Change the object specific settings, e.g. for some objects you can also set the titling, colors (for body, text and border), and border thickness if appropriate.

6. Click **Create**.

The named object will be shown in a list in the My Smart Objects Library left-hand pane. Here's an example of a selection of Smart objects, some grouped under a custom profile named Rainbow WWW Objects.

All Smart objects can be added to the page, but some Smart object types (i.e., forums or blogs) are not added to a web page but instead access Serif Web Resources directly (via offsite links or hyperlinks; see p. 36 or p. 223, respectively). The main advantage is that there is no constraint by having the Smart object contained within your page dimensions (avoiding window scrolling).

To add a Smart object to your web page:

1. From the Smart Objects dialog, select the chosen object from the left-hand pane and click the **Insert** button.

2. To insert the object at a default size, position the cursor where you want the object to appear on the page, then simply click the mouse.

The Smart object will automatically preview on the page so you'll get a good feel for how your published Smart object will look.

Editing Smart objects

Once an object is created it can be edited either in the My Smart Object Library or directly on the page. Typically, you might want to alter the appearance of the object from its original settings, maybe change a Poll question, or reset a Hit Counter back to zero.

Editing an object only affects the object itself and does not alter any collected data.

The dialog options for editing and creating a Smart object are identical.

To edit a Smart object in your library:

- From the Smart Objects dialog, click the **Edit...** button at the bottom of the My Smart Objects Library pane.

To edit a Smart object on your page:

- Double-click the object to reveal the object's Edit dialog.

If you edit an object on the web page the change is also reflected in the Objects library and vice versa.

Managing Smart objects

While editing Smart objects affects how the object operates, managing Smart objects can be used to manage the object's "gathered" data when the web page is published. Some Smart objects such as Hit Counters don't need to be managed as they just increment on each web visit (you can reset the counters though). However, other more complex Smart objects, such as Forum, Blog, User List, Poll, and Shout Box store collected visitor data such as article comments, email addresses, poll results, and a chat messaging log.

To manage a Smart object from your library:

- From the Smart Objects dialog, click the **Manage** button at the bottom of the My Smart Objects Library pane. The management options differ for each Smart object type.

See online Help for an overview of management functions.

Some of the Smart objects such as forums and blogs take more time to set up correctly. As a result, advanced help is available for each Smart object from within Serif Web Resources. A help button is located next to each Smart object in your Smart Objects Library.

To manage Smart objects directly over the Internet:

- Login to **www.serifwebresources.com** to control all your Smart objects independently of your WebPlus site. Use your usual Web Resources login as before.

Exporting Smart objects

Smart objects you've created belong to your Serif Web Resources account. However, you can export any Smart object to a different account simply. All you need is the username (email address) for that target account.

To export a selected Smart object:

- From the main Smart Objects dialog, click the **Move to Account** button at the bottom of the My Smart Objects Library pane.

- Enter the **Username**, i.e. email address, associated with the account. If you're not sure of the exact username, you can click the **Find User** button; Serif Web Resources will help you locate any existing account. If a match occurs, the dialog lets you export the file by clicking the **Move Object** button.

★ The Smart object is moved during this operation and will no longer be available from the current Serif Web Resources account.

Deleting Smart objects

To delete an object from the library:

- Select the object's entry in the My Smart Objects Library pane and click the **Delete** button. A confirmation message is displayed.

This will cause any uploaded web page which includes the object to display an empty space until the object is removed from the corresponding WebPlus's web page and the web page uploaded again.

To delete an object on your page:

- Select the object and press the **Delete** key.

Access control

Access control lets you apply security to your site, either to restrict access to specific pages or to control user access to forums and other Serif Web Resource features.

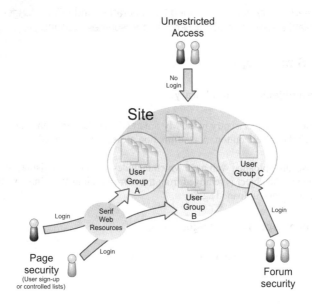

- **For page security**: login to a password-protected page(s) or via an on-the-page login box. Typically of use in personal websites or small enterprise websites, you can allow free access to most of your site, with only a limited set of pages accessible to selected web visitors. As an example, a Photo Gallery page of your family can be made "private" but still be shared with your relatives (under password control). The login details are stored in a user group associated with the page which contains a list of authorized users; the users are added manually by the web manager of the site or new users can self-register via sign up.

- **For Smart object security**: provides access control for forums and blogs (see p. 267).

  - Forums: for management of users and group moderation.

  - Blogs: for adding and removing articles via an Editors group.

Access control is possible via Serif Web Resources by using a **User List** Smart object, which can be created to manage user groups and users, and how users sign in.

> As a brief reminder, Serif Web Resources is a secure online service hosted by Serif that securely stores Smart objects (see p. 267) and any generated data. You can manage your User List Smart object, as for any other Smart object, either from within WebPlus or via **www.serifwebresources.com** at any time.

Successful establishment of access control on your website, is dependent on following the steps below.

- Setting up your User List Smart object

- Adding users (manual or self-registration)

- Enabling access control

- Adding a login box

- Advanced user control

Setting up your User List Smart object

You'll need to firstly create a User List Smart object then create one or more groups connected to that Smart object. Normally, you'll just need one Smart object per site—the individual groups can then be used to control access to specific pages or Smart object resources.

To create a User List smart object:

1. Click the **Smart Object Tool** button on the **Web Objects** toolbar.

2. Login to Serif Web Resources (See Using Smart objects; p. 267). This assumes you have a valid login; otherwise you will have to register.

3. From the dialog, select the **New...** button at the bottom of the My Smart objects Library pane.

4. In the dialog, use the scroll bar to navigate the list of Smart objects, then select **User List**, then click **OK**.

5. From the popup dialog, select **Access Control** (as opposed to Mailing List mode).

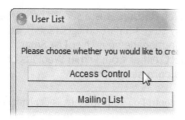

6. From the **Create Smart Object** dialog, name your Smart object and modify colors for text, buttons, background, or border, then click **Create**. Your new Smart object is listed in your Smart objects Library, e.g.

7. Click **Exit** to logout of Serif Web Resources.

Once you've created your Smart object, you can create and associate user groups to it using the Manage feature.

To control user signup and security:

1. Click ![icon] **Smart Object Tool** on the **Web Objects** toolbar.

2. With your User List Smart object selected, in the My Smart Objects Library pane, click the **Manage** button to reveal the Users dialog.

3. To switch on self-registration user sign up to the Smart object, check **Enable signups to User List**. This allows a <u>Sign up</u> link to be shown on a placed login box.

4. For extra security at user sign in, check **CAPTCHA enabled**. CAPTCHA is an anti-spamming technique where arbitrary server-generated text is displayed; the web visitor enters the text for subsequent validation.

5. Enter a redirect URL in the **Redirect after login** box if you want to direct the user to a specific web page after successful login.

6. Click **Update**.

To create a user group:

1. From the dialog, click **Groups** from the top menu.

2. From the Create New Group dialog, enter a **Group Name**; this should reflect how the group is intended to be used, e.g. "Photoaccess".

Create New Group

Group Name: Photoaccess

Add new users on signup: ☐   Automatic login/logout: ☐

3. Click the **Create Group** button, verify dialog settings, then click **Done**. The group will be added to the **Group** drop-down menu.

To manage a user group:

*   Select the group name from the **Group** drop-down menu, then click **Manage Group**.

From the dialog, you can rename the group and display the number of group users. You can make changes by clicking the **Update Group** button, or remove the group with the **Delete Group** button.

Adding users (manual or self-registration)

adding users
manually

Typically, adding users manually is great for controlled environments such as small businesses, organizations, or clubs where users are "known."

For each user group that is created, a group of **users** can be added to each user group by manual entry or import from a comma-delimited text file by the web manager.

It's possible to use either one user login (everyone uses the same login) or create a login per user for more user control (e.g., for membership lists).

self-
registration
user sign up

Conversely, user sign up is intended for more public access where controlling users is impractical—the user can simply register then sign in using their login credentials. The web manager still has the option to manage those users within their groups via the User List Smart object.

This method requires an on-screen login box to be placed on the page (normally a master page).

You can add more than one user to the same user group. The same user can belong to multiple user groups.

To add a user manually:

1. Click the **Smart Object Tool** button on the **Web Objects** toolbar.

2. With your User List Smart object selected in the My Smart objects Library pane, click the object's **Manage** button to reveal the Users dialog.

3. From the **Add New User** section at the bottom of the dialog, enter the user's email address in the **Email** box.

With **Require activation** checked, an activation link will be emailed to the user along with an auto-generated password. When unchecked, only an auto-generated password will be emailed.

With **Email User** checked, an email will be sent to the user; if unchecked, no email is sent but the user is added. The password needs to be communicated to the user via other means (telephone or verbally).

4. Click the **Add User** button. The user is added to the user list in the **Users** section.

5. To assign users to a group, click **Groups** from the top menu.

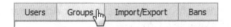

6. Select the group from the **Group** drop-down list, then add the selected user from the Users box to the Group box by clicking the **Add** button (if adding all users, click **Add All**). The user will now belong to the user group. To remove, use the **Remove** (or **Remove All**) buttons from the group.

If configured, you can make users sign up by themselves, avoiding the need to manually add and manage every user as described above. This is done via Serif Web Resources.

To enable self-registration user sign up:

This method requires a process requires a login box to be added to the master page. A new visitor to the site can sign up to become a registered user (by clicking the Sign up link on the login box).

1. Click the 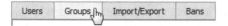 **Smart Object Tool** button on the **Web Objects** toolbar.

2. With your User List Smart object selected in the My Smart objects Library pane, click the object's **Manage** button to reveal the Users dialog.

3. Click Groups from the top menu.

Users	Groups	Import/Export	Bans

4. From the dialog, select an existing group from the **Group** drop-down list, and click **Manage Group.**

5. Check **Add new users on signup**—the user's login details on sign up will be added to the user group during registration. When checked, the sign in process allows access to **all** groups that are "sign up enabled", otherwise restricted pages will be protected.

6. Click **Update Group** and then **Done**.

★ If you're creating a new group, remember to click **Add new users on signup** in the Create New Group section.

★ Right-click an on-the-page login box and choose **Manage Smart object**.

★ When users sign up via an on-screen login box they will appear in every user group which is "user sign up enabled".

Enabling access control

To enable access control on your web page:

1. With the web page currently in view, click 🔒 **Page Security** on the Default context toolbar.

2. Check **Protect page with password** to enable access control. You'll notice that the **Change/Manage** button becomes active. Click this button to reveal currently available user groups (in bold) and the User List Smart object to which they belong.

    Photoaccess
    Rainbow_WWW

    Internal
    Rainbow_WWW

    Forum_access
    Rainbow_WWW

    Forum_access
    Outreach_WWW

3. From the User Groups dialog, select the user group, e.g. Photoaccess, then click **OK**. Your page's Page Security tab should show that the page is password protected and that the user group has been assigned.

4. Click **OK**, then **OK** again to exit the dialogs.

★ You'll now notice the page in the Site tab showing a 🔑 key symbol which indicates that page security is set.

Adding a login box

WebPlus lets you add a login/logout input box onto a page in your website. This means that a registered web visitor can gain access to any restricted pages by signing in to the site.

The login box is actually a visual representation of the User List Smart object; it is placed on the page as well as existing just in Serif Web Resources.

Users can be added manually in Serif Web Resources or via self-registration user sign up.

> ★ Add the login box to the site's master page. Any web page using the master page will then offer the user the opportunity to sign in to the website.

To add a user login box:

1. Follow the procedure under Enabling access control (see p. 283) but instead of exiting the dialog, pick a page to place your login box, then click the **Insert** button.

2. Position the **Paste** cursor where you want the user login box, then click the mouse to insert the object at a default size.

3. Enable self-registration user sign up as described previously (see p. 281).

Advanced user control

Some additional features allow you to import/export, suspend, and ban/unban users within user groups. A banned user is banned globally (access to all User Groups is prevented).

Any user can be deleted or temporarily suspended for breaking site rules (e.g., for posting defamatory statements on a hosted public forums). The next time the user tries to log on the message "Your account has been suspended" is displayed.

If more drastic action is required, a user's IP address can be banned from accessing Serif Web Resource objects (e.g., forums, etc.). As a last resort, even the ISP or organization to which the owner of the email address belongs to can be banned from access. This latter option is not recommended normally but may be necessary to prevent institutional malpractice such as professional spamming.

See online Help for more details.

Access control with forums and blogs

To set up access control for forums:

1. Select the already created User List Smart object for access control when creating a forum.

WebPlus will automatically create a user group, also called Golf Forum, to allow self-registration user sign up and sign in. The forum visitor will need to click the register link and sign up.

2. To set up a forum Moderator group, you'll need to create a moderator group, add moderators manually, manage the forum, and choose the group from the **Moderated by Group** drop-down menu.

To set up access control for blogs:

1. You'll need to create an Editors group and add editors manually.

2. Select your blog Smart object, click **Manage** and choose the newly created Editors group from the **Editors Group** drop-down menu.

13 Previewing and Publishing

Previewing your site

Previewing your site in a web browser is an essential step before publishing it to the web. It's the only way you can see just how your site will appear to a visitor. You can **preview** a page or site at any time, either within WebPlus (using an internal window based on the Internet Explorer browser) or separately using any browser installed on your system.

To preview your site:

1. Click the down arrow on the 🖳 ▾ **Preview site** button on the **Standard** toolbar.

2. Select an option from the submenu:

    *   **Preview in Window** (shortcut **Alt+P**) opens the site in a new internal WebPlus window with its own tab for convenient switching.

        When previewing in a window, you can use the Preview context toolbar to control the preview window. Click the toolbar buttons to navigate **Back** and **Forward**, **Refresh** or **Close Preview**, and redisplay the page at one of several standard or custom screen resolutions (all from a drop-down menu).

    *   Choose **Preview Page...** or **Preview Site...** to use an external browser. The names will reflect which browsers are currently installed, e.g. the entry may read "Preview Page in Internet Explorer." If you have more than one browser installed, you can select which browser(s) to display on the submenu. The page or site is exported to a temporary folder and appears in the specified browser.

To customize the list of browsers on the submenu:

1. Choose **Preview Site** from the **File** menu (or from the Preview Site flyout on the **Standard** toolbar) and select **Browser Preview List...** from the submenu.
    The dialog displays a list of browsers registered on your system. The WebPlus **Preview** submenu will list these in the order they're shown here.

2.   Use the dialog to make changes as needed:

- Click **Auto Detect** to refresh the list automatically, or click **Add** to display a dialog that lets you locate a particular browser to manually add to the list.

- To delete an entry from the list, select it and click **Remove**.

- You can rearrange the list by selecting an entry and clicking **Move Up** or **Move Down**.

- To change the entry's name on the submenu or its path, select the entry and click **Edit**. For example, you could change "Internet Explorer" to appear as simply "IE7".

3.   Click **OK** to confirm any changes.

★   It is good practise to install several of the common browsers in order to test how your site will look on an alternative system.

WebPlus allows you to view estimated download time for each page of your site, and provides information such as the number of files on each page and the total size of the files. This is useful in gaging how long it will take for each of your pages to load in various browsers, and will help you to create a site that is both quick and easy for users to navigate through.

To view estimated download time:

1.   Check that the currently displayed page is the page you want to view estimated download time for.

2.   Click the down arrow on the **Preview site** button on the **Standard** toolbar and click **Estimate download time**.

3.   The Download Time Estimation dialog displays the following information:

- **Page:** (e.g., Article 02)

- **Number of files:** (e.g., 15)

- **Total size:** (e.g., 153 KB)

- **Connection speed:** Shows download times for 56k dial-up modems or a range of different broadband connection speeds.

Publishing to the web

Publishing to the web involves uploading your site to your web host provider, turning your site into a live website, viewable by the whole world! You can specify that all web page are published or, if updating your site, only pages changed since the last "publish."

Before publishing to the web, it is worth checking for potential problems by running the Site Checker (**Tools>Site Manager>Site Checker...**).

> Remember that you can publish to disk folder at any time, which lets you test your website offline (and locally) before publishing to web. See online Help for more details.

To publish your site to the web:

1. Choose **Site Properties...** from the **File** menu and double-check export settings, particularly those on the Graphics tab.

2. Click the 🔳 **Publish site** button on the **Standard** toolbar (or choose **Publish Site** from the **File** menu and select **Publish to Web...** from the submenu).

If this is your first time publishing to the web, you'll see a **Publish to Web** dialog without any account information present (you'll see your local site ready to upload). You'll need to set up at least one account before you can proceed.

1. Click the **Accounts...** button to display the **Upload to Server** dialog.

2. Click **Add...**

3. In the **Account Details** dialog, enter:

    - The **Account name**. This can be any name of your choice. You'll use it to identify this account in WebPlus (in case you have more than one).

- The **FTP address** of your web host will be a specific URL starting with "ftp://" as supplied by your service provider.

- **Port number**: Unless directed by your provider, you can leave this set at "21."

- Leave the **Folder** box blank unless directed by your provider, or if you want to publish to a specific subfolder of your root directory.

- You'll also need a **Username** and **Password** as pre-assigned by the provider. Most likely these will correspond to email login settings. Be sure to enter the password exactly as given to you, using correct upper- and lower-case spelling, or the host server may not recognize it.

- Check **Save password** to record the password on your computer, if you don't want to re-enter it with each upload.

- **Passive mode**: Leave checked unless you have FTP connection problems (check with your ISP). ISPs can operate passive or active FTP modes of operation.

- **Web site URL**: Set your site's URL. This allows you to view the web site from a dialog after FTP upload.

- In the **Advanced** box, you can optionally enable Secure FTP by uploading using one of two encryption protocols—TLS 1.0 and SSL 3.0. Check **Encrypt connection**, then choose the **Protocol**. You'll need to confirm with your ISP whether encryption (and which protocol) is supported, implied or otherwise. The **SSL Implied** option makes the ISP's FTP server encrypt on initial contact to default port 990 or a custom port (edit Port number).

- Click **OK** to close Account Details.

You can also use the Upload to Server dialog at this point to **Add...** another account, and **Copy...**, **Edit** or **Delete** an account selected from the drop-down menu. It's a good idea to test your new or modified account by clicking the **Test** button—if the test is successful a dialog will display stating that a connection has been established.

You can choose to Save FTP account details either to your machine (account details will be saved into WebPlus and won't be lost, even after Ctrl-Runup) or into the current site.

4. If you've set up at least one account and clicked the **Update Account...** button, the **Publish to Web** dialog appears with the last used account name shown in the drop-down menu and its settings in subsequent boxes. The drop-down menu lets you swap to another account. Select the account you want to use (if you've more than one).

5. For the greatest control over the publishing, ensure that the **Unattended upload** check box is cleared. This will allow you to review the changes that will take place to your published website before they are made. It will also give you the option to cancel the upload if you discover a problem. (See Automatic Operation on p. 295 for more details on this feature.)

6. Choose which pages you want to upload—check specific page(s) in the window or **Publish All Pages**. Use the **Toggle Select**, **Toggle Branch** and **Select All** buttons to aid page selection.

7. To safeguard your WebPlus site, check the **Backup the document to the remote server** option. If the site is unsaved you'll be prompted to save it.

8. Click **OK**. WebPlus seeks an Internet connection, then:

9. If uploading for the first time, selected files will be uploaded directly.

    -or-

    If uploading to an existing site, an Uploading Files dialog is displayed showing local file action (whether files will be added (Add), will replace the live file (Replace) or not updated (Leave)).

    In the dialog, check the option to Delete unused remote files if you want WebPlus to automatically remove any unused graphic and page files.

    Select either the **Incremental Update** or **Full upload** Button. Choose the former to upload only files that have altered since the last upload. When doing an incremental update, you can get WebPlus to **Check for missing files** by checking the option box. However, as this can dramatically slow the upload, this option is unchecked by default.

You'll see a message when all files have been successfully copied. Click **OK**.

10. From the drop-down menu in the Website Publishing dialog, select the browser in which you wish to view your live site and click **View this URL**. You will now be able to view your live site.

If you rename/delete files and then republish one or a few pages to the web, the old files are not deleted automatically so you'll need to delete these manually by using **Publish Site>Maintain Website...** on the **File** Menu. However, if you republish the whole site to the web automatically (using Automatic Operation), you can choose to delete any unused files; check the **Delete unused files** check box.

Handling FTP account information

WebPlus gives the web developer the option of saving your FTP account details either on your machine or in the current site, or both. Account details are kept on the computer by default, but by saving details within your site you can transfer your site to another machine without losing your account details and then republish from there.

★ Password details are never stored in sites for security reasons.

An additional option allows you to export **all** FTP account details (including passwords) onto a different computer.

To save FTP account details in your site:

1. From the **Publish to Web** dialog, click **Accounts...**.

2. In the dialog's Save FTP account details section, check **Into current site**.

3. Click **Update Account**.

When the site is opened on another machine, the details will still only be stored on the site. You can optionally check the **On this machine** option to store the account details on the machine as well as in the site.

To export all FTP account details:

1. From the **Publish to Web** dialog, click **Accounts...**.

2. In the dialog's FTP Account section, click **Export All**.

3. Choose a location and file name for the registry file (.reg), then click **Save**.

4. Transfer the .reg file to a different computer, then double-click the file.

> ⚠ Any existing FTP accounts on the target computer will be overwritten.

Automatic Operation

If you have a very large website, you may want to use the Automatic Operation feature. The actual process is virtually the same as Publish to Web but it allows you to upload the site without having to "OK" each dialog that may appear. This is especially useful if you are updating a site containing a large database with images.

1. Check **Unattended upload.** This also enables the following options;

    *   Check **Use incremental upload** to only replace files that have changed from the last upload (if you've already published the website to the same FTP folder previously), which is an efficient method of uploading since there are less files to transfer.

        With this enabled you can also select **Check remote files** to prompt WebPlus to manually check each file before replacing it. This decreases the speed of uploading compared to normal operation but is a more thorough method of publishing.

    *   Check **Delete unused files** to remove files from the FTP folder that aren't needed for the website you are publishing (e.g., this is relevant when you upload a completely different website to your FTP folder).

2. Choose which pages you want to upload—check specific page(s) in the window or **Publish All Pages**. Use the **Toggle Select**, **Toggle Branch** and **Select All** buttons to aid page selection.

3. To safeguard your site, check the **Backup the document to the remote server** option. If the site is unsaved you'll be prompted to save it.

4. Click **OK** to begin the upload process. (Now is the time to get that cup of tea...)

5. Once the upload is complete, the Uploading files dialog will remain on screen until you click **Close**.

6. From the drop-down menu in the Website Publishing dialog, select the browser in which you wish to view your live site and click **View this URL**. You will now be able to view your live site.

Trouble Shooting

After publishing your website, you may find that some changes are missing. Before you attempt to do another upload, try clearing the cache on your browser. To clear the cache, press **Ctrl+F5**. This will often cure any problems relating to the display of images and other objects.

If clearing the cache doesn't resolve the problems, you may need to manually delete old image files or objects. See Maintaining your website in online Help for details on how to do this.

Viewing your published site

Once your site has been published, you have the option to   **View Site Online** on the **Standard** toolbar. This displays your site in its most recently published state in the default web browser. The first time View site online is used, a dialog pops up asking for the default site URL. This can be amended later using the **Site Properties...** dialog.

It is important to remember that any changes made since publishing will not be reflected. To see unpublished changes, use the **Preview site** button. (See Previewing your site on p. 289.)

Serif provides competitively priced web hosting that offers various levels of service to suit your individual requirements. See Using Serif web hosting on p. 298 for more details.

Quick Publish

Quick Publish allows you to quickly upload and view the currently displayed page—useful for live verification of individual pages as you build your website. In order for Quick Publish to function, you must first setup your account details using the Quick Publish Configuration dialog.

To configure Quick Publish:

1. Click the **Publish site** flyout on the **Standard** toolbar and then click **Quick Publish Configure**.

    -or-

    Click **File>Publish Site>Quick Publish Configuration...**

2. In the dialog,

    - Enter the details of, or select from the drop-down menu, the URL of the site you want to publish to.

    - Select the browser in which you wish to view your page once it has been published.

    - Select the FTP account you want to use from the drop-down menu. To update account settings, or add a new account, click **Manage Accounts**.

    It's a good idea to test your new or modified account by clicking the **Test** button—if the test is successful a dialog will display stating that a connection has been established.

3. Click **OK**.

To Quick Publish to Web:

- Click the **Publish site** flyout on the **Standard** toolbar and then click **Quick Publish to Web**.

    -or-

    Click **File>Publish Site>Quick Publish to Web.**

If you attempt to use Quick Publish without configuring your account settings first, the Quick Publish Configuration dialog will automatically open for you to do so.

The Uploading Files dialog briefly appears before your page is displayed in your chosen browser.

Using Serif web hosting

Serif web hosting provides Serif-supplied web space for the user to publish to. By signing up to the hosting service you can simplify web publishing with the option of upgrading your web hosting capabilities over time.

Some of the main advantages of Serif web hosting include:

- **Simple setup.** Your web hosting account details are transferred to WebPlus in a single-click. Publishing is quick and easy.

- **Free hosting** and **email address** for a limited period.

- **Hosting via Serif Web Resources**. This means that you can access and change account details via the web (and not WebPlus), while managing your hosted Smart objects.

Serif web hosting requires that you have a working Serif Web Resources login (see Using Smart objects on p. 267). If you're not already a registered user you must create a Web Resources account first.

Serif offers a range of additional web hosting packages for purchase, each offering increasing levels of service including higher transfer limits, more disk spaces, unrestricted domain naming, and email account support. Contact Serif for details.

To activate web hosting (via WebPlus):

1. Either

   - Click the 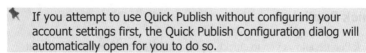 **Smart Objects Tool** on the **Web Objects** toolbar.

   - In the dialog, click **My Hosting**, select the browser in which you wish to view your page once it has been published.

OR

- Click the ![icon] **Publish site** button on the **Standard** toolbar (or choose **Publish Site** from the **File** menu and select **Publish to Web...** from the submenu).

- In the dialog, click **WebPlus.net Hosting...**.

2. From the Serif Web Resources dialog, choose various hosting option according to requirements:

   - Choose a password.

   - (Optional) Input your supplied **Coupon code** for your web hosting package (if purchased as an upgrade).

   - Select your **Region** (e.g., Europe, North America, etc.). This is the region in which your website will be hosted, so if you're targeting European users keep with the Europe option.

3. Click **Create Hosting**.

Your site can now be uploaded via **Publish site>Publish to Web** or **Publish site>Quick Publish to Web** on the **Standard** toolbar.

⚲ If you have an FTP account already set up as default in WebPlus, the new Serif web hosting account will become the new default. See Setting site properties (Publishing tab) on p. 54.

14 Index

Notes